Voices *from* Room 6

Voices *from* Room 6

a teacher remembers

Keep hope Alive
Paul J. O'Brien

Paul J. O'Brien

Permission granted by *The English Record* to print the following three essays:

"A Lesson." Originally appeared as "Sacrifice in a One-Room Schoolhouse." *The English Record.* 64 (Spring 2014) 16-19. Print.

"Discovery." Originally appeared as "Driftwood." *The English Record.* 66 (Fall/Winter 2015) 71-74. Print.

"The Wire Walker." Originally appeared as "Learning Magic with Philippe Petit." *The English Record.* 63 (Spring 2013) 46-52. Print. 6

Voices From Room 6: A Teacher Remembers

Book and Cover design by Nicholas Alberti
& The Troy Book Makers

Printed in the United States of America

The Troy Book Makers • Troy, New York
thetroybookmakers.com

ISBN: 978-1-61468-320-9

Dedication

To Deborah who has been steadfast and generous always.

To my family - Anna, Harold, Leo, Rose, John, Colin - who always encouraged me to be the best teacher I could be.

To the Notre Dame Sisters and the Edmund Rice Brothers who gave me the chance to teach and showed me their love of Christ.

To all my teachers, both in the classroom and in my life, who helped me to see the way more clearly.

To all those students whom I was privileged to teach for 47 years.

Special thanks to Rick Pepe, whose book *Thank You For My Children* and whose advice served as beacons for my own book. Much appreciation to my editors: Deborah, Patti Rand, Carolyn Nadeau, Robert Wood, Rich Holt and Andrea Sheeran. A strong thank you to Joe Malinowski for technical assistance and to Dan Pepe for his photography.

Foreword

I'm in the back seat of my father's 1947 Buick being driven by my older brother, Leo, a seminarian studying for the priesthood. In the front seat next to Leo is my younger brother, John, the top of his head barely visible from the back seat. I don't know why Leo is home from the seminary, nor do I know why John and I are out of school. I do recall feeling the warm sun on my face and arm as I gaze out the open back window. And then the image. We are stopped at a red light. I look directly into a school yard. The time must be about mid-day for there are students sitting on steps eating lunches, and students casually strolling on the grounds talking and laughing. And under one large tree stands a man maybe in his late 30's wearing a tan sport coat. He has a couple of books under his arm, and he is surrounded by students. From where I sit, I cannot hear the spoken words, but I can see clearly that both he and they are laughing over something just said. The light changes. The image remains fixed in my mind.

Another image. The sound of my mother's voice. Reading to me and my brother at bedtime. Within moments, John is asleep, but I am awake, listening to her read the lives of the Saints. St. Isaac Jogues and Rene Goupil at Auriesville. The stoning of St. Stephen. The missionaries and their unselfish dedication, epitomized most in my memory by Francis Xavier.

These two images and their effect on me are forever connected with the two people who had the greatest influence on the direction of my life and my choice of career. It was as if Leo drove me past life's possibilities while my mother's voice grounded me in stories and in the Faith.

Closing Shop

I did not remove anything from my classroom until exams were done. I knew that in many ways the dismantling of the room would be the most difficult thing I did in closing out my teaching career. A close second was the moment in the hallway when the academic dean asked me if he should put me in the slots for the following year on the master schedule. I said that he should fill those slots with another teacher. He paused, "Really?" And I said, "Yes." The final step though seemed more definitive. All classrooms reflect the teacher who teaches in that room. After many years of teaching - I had been in Room 6 for over 25 years - and prior to that down the hallway so that I had just transported all my paraphernalia with me - the reflection becomes layered and complex. Dante places hoarders in Circle Four of the *Inferno*: no question, I am a hoarder. Yet, like many hoarders, I can make an argument for every item in my room as having significance. Many have been part of my teaching world for years and years. Each one has some link to the literature and the values I have tried to convey to my students. Each one tells a story.

A Lesson, An Awakening, A Discovery

Lesson

A one-room school house - eight grades in one room, each row a grade. As a high school teacher for most of my life, I still marvel at how one teacher could possibly have taught eight grades, an entire school program, in one room. When I think of my first one-room schoolhouse (I attended two), my memory is triggered by the thought of two moments. The first year I recall that I was the only student who couldn't look at the camera for the official school photograph: the photographer was exasperated at my tear-filled eyes, and the teacher turned me sideways and stuck a book in my hand. The title was *Health for Young Americans.*

Grade two offered me my first existential crisis, although I didn't realize it at the time. On a warm, spring Friday, I opened my lunch bag to the dreaded egg salad sandwich. Because we were Catholic and because it was Lent, my mother made sure that we never had meat on Friday. It seemed that her favorite Friday sandwich was egg salad. I despised egg salad - I didn't like the way the egg looked, the texture of the white globs, the smell. Still

I settled into the lunchtime routine: we sat at our desks eating our lunches - my sandwich lay hidden inside my lunch bag - and the rule was that when everyone was done, we were allowed to go out to the playground, the chief rewards, the four swings that faced the school and the two adjacent teeter-totters.

I sat in the second seat in the second row - thinking. I had come up with a plan to rid myself of the dreaded sandwich. When the teacher disappeared into the coat room, I popped out of my desk and dropped my wax-paper covered sandwich into the trash can next to the teacher's desk. Did she have x-ray vision? Because when she emerged from the coat room, it seemed to me that she marched directly to the trash can and stared into it. With one dramatic gesture, she reached down and pulled out the sandwich.

"Who did this? she asked. "Who threw this sandwich out?" She glared at the class. "No one goes out to play until the one who threw this sandwich out confesses."

Stillness. Time had stopped. My heart was racing. "I did it," came a soft voice from the first row. To my disbelief, it was my brother John, a year and a half younger, who sat in the fourth seat in the first row.

From high on a swing outside, I could see my brother sitting in a desk in the first row with the teacher standing over him.

On the walk home, once out of the teacher's listening range, I got right to the point. "You didn't throw that sandwich away." John stopped and looked directly at me. "How do you know?" he asked. "Because I did!" He stared at me. "Why did you admit it?" I said. "Because," he responded, "I didn't think that everyone should have to stay in for what one person did." I said something like, "Boy, are you dumb! That's stupid." And we continued our walk home.

A few years later in a school with one teacher per grade, my seventh grade class was discussing the idea of sacrifice and the notion of accepting suffering to alleviate the pain of others. It was then that I thought of my brother and his gesture in the one-room schoolhouse.

Many years later, when I was well into my teaching career and my brother was a physician in Boston, I wrote a poem commemorating this moment and sent it to him.

"Sacrifice in a One-room Schoolhouse"

She saw in the depths
of the trash can
the egg salad sandwich
wrapped in waxed paper.
Swooping down
she seized it and brought it up.
"All right! Who did it?"

She roared.

"The sandwich in the trash!"
"Who put this sandwich
in the trash?"

I was frozen.
She held the sandwich
in her right hand
a rejected gift.

"No one goes out to play
until the culprit confesses!"

"No one!"

Cold silence
and a burning glare.

"I did it. It was mine."
A faint voice
but a confession.
The criminal -
a frail first grader.
"All right. Everyone
outside for play.
John, you will remain
in your seat."

From high on the swing outside

I could see my brother
sitting patiently
and accepting the blame
for something
someone else had done.
He didn't know
that his sacrifice
had been for his brother.

Awakening

On a hot summer day many years ago, my mother, splattered with flour and fingers thick with pie dough, called me into the kitchen and said, "Paul, run up to Spruksie's (local store) and get me a five pound bag of sugar. I don't think I have enough for these pies. Take a few dollars from the top of my dresser." Even though it was a hot summer day, I felt like Brer Rabbit heading for the briar patch. For about an eighth of a mile down the road, there was Baker's Garage, where small bottles of Coke floated among big chunks of ice and Hershey Bars sat on a shelf just waiting for me to select one. With change from the store, my rewards would come on the way home. A soda and a Hershey Bar were only 5 cents each.

And so I began the walk into the small village of Raymertown - we were at one end of the town and the store was at the other. Route 7 is a major highway, but cars on hot summer days seemed infrequent. I passed Ward's where we played baseball and waved to Mr. Baker, who was just crawling out from under a car. As I approached the Minister's Field, another venue for baseball, I saw a car parked on my side of the road - there was room for the car and for me to get around it. As I walked by, I heard a voice, "Heh, Son, where you going?" I looked into the car and saw a tall man sitting in the driver's seat. "To the store," I said. "Would you like a ride?" he asked. And because it was a hot summer day, I said, "Sure" and got in.

The car didn't move. Instead a series of questions that seemed to come in a kind of slow rhythm: "What's your name, son?"; "Where do you live?"; "Where were you going?" I don't recall turning to look at him; rather I stared ahead at the store in the distance. The car had the old sofa seat, and I have a vague recollection that at some point his right arm had stretched over in my direction. I remember feeling cold. "Do you have brothers?" he asked. I remember saying yes. "How many?" I said, "Two, one younger, the other older." The next question left me lost. "Have you ever seen them nude?" I said, "My younger brother." I can't remember the exact question - maybe "What did he look like?" My words were having difficulty coming out, "Like any other boy," I think I said. I remember at this point that I started praying the prayer that my mother had taught me, a prayer that was the heart of the family rosary - the Hail Mary. And adding, "Jesus, please help me."

He started the car and pulled out onto the road. "Jesus, please make him stop the car," I kept repeating as the store loomed closer. The car began to pick up speed. And then, "Thank you, Jesus," as he started to slow down. Near the store, he pulled over in a space meant for a few cars. I reached for the handle and opened the door. "See you again sometime, Paul." As he pulled away, for some reason, I kept my head down until I reached the door of the store. I walked inside and said, "Mr. Spruks, I was supposed to buy something, but I can't remember what it was and something bad just happened." And then I ran out the exit and didn't stop until I was back in my mother's kitchen.

Words and tears poured out together - I seem to remember my mother holding my hands. "There was this guy, stopped in the village, by the Minister's Field, and he asked me if I wanted a ride, and I said yes." As soon as I had finished, my mother called my father, who worked for the New York State Highway Department. It seemed that within minutes a State Trooper was knocking at the door. I remember he had many questions about the appearance of the man, the make of his car, the things he said. I remember crying again as I told my story. When I was done, the trooper spoke softly to my mother and then looked down at me. "Paul, from this point on, never get into a car with a stranger. Remember that - it's very important."

Over the years, I have come to reflect on how lucky I was. How close had this man come to abusing me and maybe worse? I was fortunate that day in our simple country town with the sun shining and me on my way to buy sugar for my Mom's apple pies. It was a bright summer day, but darkness was out there.

Discovery

On a chartered bus trip from London to Stratford, the bus driver turned to me in the front seat and said, "You know, the great thing about getting out of the city is that it gives you a chance to exercise the eyes - in London, you can't see very far with all those buildings." The bus driver's words, I think, can also apply to the meaning of summer for teachers. Away from the city of formal education, summer gives teachers a chance to "exercise the eyes." Through travel and reading and serenity, we can return a little healthier, strengthened by summer's offerings.

At the family house on Raquette Lake, I am lounging on the dock and gazing at two pieces of driftwood on the front lawn. The smaller and more interesting piece - like a prehistoric bird in a moment of repose or an Olympic diver frozen in flight - rests on the wooden cover of the house's well.

"Know anything about the driftwood on the well?" I say to my wife who is immersed in a British mystery novel.

After about ten seconds, she looks up, "Driftwood?" I point at the well. "I don't know. Probably Buddy picked it up from the shoreline."

As she returns to her book, I say, "You know, I think I'd like to find a piece of driftwood for my classroom. Maybe bring a little of Raquette Lake to Room 6."

"Beer anyone?" says my brother-in-law, who has been dozing on the dock and now starts to get up.

"Sounds great," I say and add, "Heh, Hen, what do you think about helping me find a piece of driftwood for my classroom. That would be so cool."

"Sure," he says, "we can take the small boat into Pug Bay. There's probably some really good stuff over there. Not sure what you will do with it though."

Having Henry navigate the boat is somewhat akin to having my own Adirondack guide. Now in his mid-thirties, he's been exploring Raquette Lake for over twenty summers. In Pug Bay, the water has become quite shallow, and he has tilted the motor so that it doesn't strike any rocks. We are on the Forever Wild side of the lake, and it is very quiet, even eerie. Something very dark seems to move down in the water. For a second or two, my paranoid side allows Stephen King to enter my mind. I stare into the water. Now stillness. I get a grip on myself, look up and scan the shoreline. So many trees along the shore have parts that have been ripped off and are mangled, revealing the harsh effects of wind and rain and the unmerciful Adirondack winter. The ground and shore water are littered with the white and greying bones of trees. I think of Adelaide Crapsey's poem "On Seeing Weather-Beaten Trees." The poem takes the form of a question: "Is it as plainly in our living shown,/ by slant and twist which way the winds have blown?" (Crapsey Modern American Poetry).

"How about that one?" Henry asks, pointing to a partially submerged piece of driftwood about fifteen feet away. I keep expecting to see one of the big logs near the driftwood turn into an enormous snake. "Looks pretty good," I say.

He eases the boat up close and reaches down to lift the driftwood out of the water. The submerged section, though somewhat frail in appearance, is much more interesting than I expected. Like some ancient lake creature, whose head Henry now holds in his right hand, it appears to have risen to scan the lake. Its body is gnarled and cracked. Rising from the back is a narrow fin that twists and intersects with another fin that seems to ripple back to the broken tail of the creature. Beneath the intersecting fins, a third fin rises but is cut off. Below this third fin is a small curved arc that seems to serve as an entrance way into a dark space. Henry places the wood down carefully in the boat and says, "Yeah, that's a good one."

Back home in Niskayuna, the sun's light is slipping away from the steer's horns that is the driftwood drying in our back yard. As my eyes move downward, the driftwood seems to become arms that cross and twist reminding me of Laocoon and his two sons snared in Book II of Virgil's *Aeneid*. Twilight touches the grayness of the wood and makes the wood seem for a moment a harbinger of fog. Time to move it into the garage for the night.

The bus driver was right. Once you move out of your confined and familiar world, you can begin to see more clearly. With the help of a guide or your own inquisitive spirit, you can discover new worlds. And once the world emerges, then your imagination can begin to marvel and create. A piece of driftwood in a classroom, an echo of another world and time. Perhaps it will give the students pause. And then, what stories and poems may rise up while gazing at a piece of driftwood from Raquette Lake?

Two Artists Who Graced My Life

The Surfer

In the far left corner high on the shelf behind my desk, a surfer, tall with a natural grace, rides a wave off the coast of Montauk. There was another wave a few years earlier that the same surfer rode. A friend recalls the moment: "The tide was low and flowing fast. It was bigger than it looked. The first few waves took us by surprise. I had just gotten outraced, and as I retrieved my board, I saw the next one coming up the line, maybe fifty yards, already grinding and pitching. Tucker moved out to meet it. It was doubling up and thick. I paddled hard for the horizon. He didn't have a chance, but Tucker turned and took it. This wave was gunning for him. I knew I had to focus on my escape, but I was mesmerized. He accelerated, climbing and dropping high under the curl. Each turn was slightly behind, slightly late, right on the outer edge of control. He couldn't quite get ahead of it. He moved like a fencer. It was beautiful to see. The wave was relentless. He flew towards me, and as I neared the crest, I looked back at Tucker tucked deep in the oncoming vortex. He wasn't going to make it.... It was a powerful moment of poise and imminent failure. The last thing I saw as I went over the top was that he was out-done and turned sharply for the beach. It didn't last ten seconds. There were better waves to come that day, and I am sure he forgot that one. But I thought it was great, and it stuck in my memory. He rode with such heart, and his calm intensity expressed something valiant in his spirit" (Pomianowski).

Tucker Geery - husband, father, carpenter, surfer. On the front page of the program from his funeral, Tucker stands tall in front of the last house he helped build, smiling. Inside the program, there is another picture of Tucker surfing a much more menacing wave than the one in the picture on my shelf, with his friend's testimony superimposed over the wave. In this image and action, Tucker radiates a kind of epic hero, trying to ride as best he can the ocean of experience. His action here and in his town of Montauk served as a modern parallel for me in helping to illuminate Book 22 of Homer's *Odyssey*. Odysseus - King, husband, father, traveler, warrior. Odysseus, ten years riding his own ocean of experience trying to find his way home.

The last picture I had of Tucker was sent to me by Kathryn, his wife and my niece, from Sloan-Kettering Hospital, where he had been taken to ease the growing pain from his cancer. "If Tucker were awake, he never would have let me take this picture," said Kathy. In the picture, Tucker looks peaceful, his right hand under the right side of his face. In his left hand, which is resting on his left hip, he holds a rosary, something that had pretty much been with him from the moment he received it. "Show Josh this picture," Kathy had said.

Early in the fall of the previous year, Josh had come up to me after class and said, "Can I give Tucker my rosary?" I had been praying each day for Tucker in my classes. A stocky, strong-willed senior, Josh had battled many demons on his journey. Abandoned by his own family, Josh had been adopted by a family in the school, and they had given him a rosary, which they had gotten from Medjugorje, Herzegovina, where the Blessed Virgin Mary had appeared. Josh valued it highly. "That is very thoughtful of you," I said to him. "Let me check with Kathy and see." After talking with Kathy, I told Josh that he could mail the rosary to Tucker.

On the day the rosary arrived, Tucker's younger daughter was on her way home early from Scotland, where she had been living as part of her study-abroad program. Tucker did not know that she would be coming home early. The rosary arrived, and a few hours later Simone appeared in the doorway, to her father's surprise and delight. For the next few months, the rosary always stayed close to Tucker.

Kathy had met Tucker shortly after she had moved to Montauk. She was hitch-hiking back to her apartment, and Tucker stopped to pick her up in his beat-up truck. The relationship was sealed almost instantly. Tall with long blond hair, Tucker could have been stereotyped as surfer-guy, which he was - a very good surfer. But he was also blessed with carpentry and building skills, a strong work ethic, an incredibly gentle spirit, and a most engaging smile. A carpenter by trade, Tucker was a native to Montauk and knew the people and that world very well.

Fishermen, surfers, blue collar laborers - Montauk was a world totally unlike the Hamptons where money flashed and Ralph Lauren was ubiquitous. Tucker loved Montauk. As his good friend, Russell Drumm, pointed out, Montauk was a unique community. Speaking about Tucker's last days, he said, "We were all praying for Tucker's suffering to end. By 'we,' I mean the tribe, the wave of people, surfers, fishermen, carpenters, who in the late 1960s and early 70s found our way to Montauk, joined the locals, became friends, and as the years passed, evolved into family" (Drumm B1).

And then Russell told a story that revealed what the Montauk world meant to Tucker. In late autumn of 1972, Tucker and the regulars were in their favorite Montauk watering hole, the Shagwong. They were dancing, singing, and drinking when a motorcycle gang called the Pagans barged into the tavern. One of them threw a shot glass through the stained glass behind the bar; another punched a middle-aged woman as she tried to exit, knocking her to the floor. "The next thing I know, Tucker - mild mannered, funny, ever-smiling - had his face inches from the biker's mug. Tucker looked fierce, his eyes boring into those of the Pagan. Everything got quiet. I remember thinking, 'Well, this is it. Get ready.' Then I heard Tucker speaking through clinched teeth. 'Don't ever come here again,' he told the guy. The Pagan responded, 'Why the hell not?' Tucker said, 'Because next time, we will be waiting at the Overlook.'" (The Overlook was a high point in the terrain where the Montauk Indians would gather to defend themselves against enemy tribes.)

Drumm said that it was like a line from an old western, "Like Tucker was channeling Gary Cooper." It worked. The biker backed down. After a bit more bluster, the gang left and the clash was over. In reflecting on the incident, Drumm was struck by the fearlessness that had erupted from his peaceful friend. He knew of Tucker's easygoing strength from his surfing, for Tucker had ridden the biggest wave to ever reach Montauk. But his final reflection hit the heart of the matter. "Tucker believed in our Montauk community. I think he believed in it so much that when it was threatened that night his word instinctively placed us at the ramparts, to the highlands above the only road into town... I think Tucker lived much of his life on the Overlook, looking over and after his friends, his wife,

Kathryn, and his beloved daughters. Sunday morning, when I learned of his passing, I realized how much I owe this soft-spoken, fearless friend" (Star B4).

And so Tucker's moment is shared with my students after we have read of Odysseus's arrow flying through the twelve ax heads and then listened to Odysseus speak - the first time in twenty years as Ithaca's King. He stands in front of the suitors, those disreputable miscreants who have almost destroyed his home, cruelly treated his wife Penelope, and threatened to kill his son. He is now no longer the beggar that Athena insisted he become if he was to be successful at defeating the suitors and regaining his home. Odysseus, transformed by Athena into the King of Ithaca, says, "You yellow dogs, you thought I'd never make it home from the land of Troy. You took my house to plunder, twisted my maids to serve your bed. You dared bid for my wife while I was still alive. Contempt was all you had for the gods who rule wide heaven, contempt for what men say of you hereafter. Your last hour has come. You die in blood" (Homer *Odyssey* 410).

In the past I have used other media to parallel what Odysseus is feeling: the movie *Carrie* speaks to the issue when she is cruelly treated by having pig's blood poured over her at the prom, and she responds with her telekinetic powers; the movie *Superman II* when Clark Kent, now restored in power, settles things in the diner with the bully who had beaten him up earlier. But Tucker's action and words offer a closer parallel. In both Tucker's case and Odysseus's, their worlds have been threatened by dark forces; in each case, each man takes a stand and defends what is most important to him: his world. In life and in literature, moral strength wins the day.

After Tucker's funeral, my niece mailed the rosary back to Josh with a note saying how important it had been to Tucker. Yes, the rosary had been a pretty special gift, and Josh had risen above my expectations and showed his magnanimous spirit. In Tucker's painful struggle to his end, Josh had lightened the journey and had also taken on the characteristic of a hero.

The Wire Walker

On the morning of August 7, 1974, Philippe Petit, a high-wire artist, stepped out on a cable, rigged between the North Tower and the South Tower of the World Trade Center. For the next 45 minutes, he crossed the cable eight times and would have been there longer had he not been threatened by police and told that a helicopter would snatch him off the wire. In that marvelous feat of skill and poetry - Philippe actually performed on the cable - he became an indelible cultural icon. In the 2003 Caldecott Award winning illustrated book, "The Man Who Walked Between the Towers," by Mordicai Gerstein, and in the 2008 Academy Award Documentary, *Man on Wire,* Philippe's accomplishment is celebrated.

I knew that the movie had captured the seniors. I knew during the film because not one of the students had walked by me heading to the bathroom or to the lobby for more candy, soda or popcorn. When they filed by me on the way out of the theater, they walked almost as if they were spellbound; legitimately in awe.

The Spectrum Theater, an outstanding venue for documentaries and independent films, had sent a notice to area schools a few weeks earlier that there were special showings of *Man on Wire* available for students. Philippe Petit had been a cultural hero in my mind since his miraculous walk between the Two Towers. The Towers had taken on personal meaning for me in the 80's when my wife's downstate law office was in the South Tower. Traveling to the City with her, I had been to the observation deck a number of times to gaze at the splendor of New York. Since 2003, I had been reading to the students in the senior elective Popular Culture, as an example of a modern heroic feat, Mordicai Gerstein's "The Man Who Walked Between the Towers," a beautifully illustrated story of Philippe's walk.

The bus ride back to the school was charged with animated discussion about how amazing Philippe's accomplishment was. References to all the obstacles Philippe and his team had to overcome danced in the air: hiding from the guards, standing perfectly still under a tarp for hours, almost losing the arrow, accidentally letting the cable fall so that it had to be lugged back up painstakingly, enough to exhaust anyone, and the cloudy, overcast day. And yet he had done it. Philippe had walked for nearly an hour on the cable, eight crossings. Yes, they were in awe. It was an awesome accomplishment.

"Can we write him about how the movie affected us," implored a student the following day in class. Since all had gone to the film, I asked each of my three senior classes if they wanted to write Philippe and speak of their experience of his walk. Amazingly, not one student objected.

The following day, the students spent the class composing letters to Philippe, some with questions, some just detailing what they found so overwhelming. One student wondered if Philippe might ever come and visit us. I read through the letters that night, then placed the 52 letters in a manila envelope, along with my letter, and the following day mailed them to Philippe at St. John the Divine Church in Manhattan, where I had learned that he was artist in residence.

Anyone who has taught for a while knows how eager students are to have immediate responses to their writing. Each day in class would begin with, "Have you heard anything?" And, "Do you know if he got the letters?" And, "Would he ever write back?"

After three weeks of being beleaguered by students - though their enthusiasm was waning - I called St. John the Divine and asked to speak to Philippe. I was connected to a public relations person who was friendly and understanding. He told me that Philippe had received the letters and was very touched, but that he was a very private person and probably wouldn't be responding. I thanked him, and the following day I told the students that he had received the letters and had been moved, but that they should not expect any response from him.

Roughly two weeks later, my wife, while reading the paper, noticed that St. John the Divine was having a rededication ceremony after a period of renovation following a fire in the Church. What jumped out at her was the fact that Philippe was going to perform a one-man show that day as part of the celebration. She asked me if I wanted to go. The following Saturday we were on Amtrak heading to the City.

Philippe entered our circle on a unicycle at about the mid-point of the Church. Dressed in black and wearing his stove-pipe hat, he performed a series of mimes, interacting creatively and humorously with the audience, and then did a series of juggling acts. The most dramatic moment came after he had called four men out of the audience. Taking a scarf from one man, he folded it neatly and placed it back on the man's shoulder. Then he lined the other men up behind the first one. Taking a rope from his black bag, he placed one end on the scarfed shoulder and extended the rope back to the other men lined up behind. Next he walked away from the men about 40-50 feet to a church column and attached the rope to a steel pin in the column. Climbing up a small ladder near the column, he stepped onto the rope - now maybe five feet above the floor. And he began walking. Step by step he moved toward the men - the rope swaying significantly from side to side. When he reached the man with the scarf on his shoulder, he kept one foot on the rope, the other gently touched the chest of the man. Then Philippe lifted both arms in a victorious gesture. Leaping to the floor, he gathered his rope, placed it in his bag, and bicycled out of the circle of people. I remember thinking that I had just seen my second amazing feat from this man.

Looking at my wife, I shook my head in disbelief - uttering something like, "Whew." I knew that the trip had been worth it just to see that walk. As we prepared to depart, Debbie said that she needed to use the ladies' room, and I sat down in a pew to relax and think about the day. The line had been lengthy, and she returned in about fifteen minutes. As we made our way out of the back of the Church, I spotted Philippe talking with two people. I looked at Debbie and said, "I am going to introduce myself." I stood a respectable distance until I saw the people reaching out to shake hands good-bye. I stepped forward quickly and put out my hand. He responded with his hand and a smile. After telling him I had loved his performance, I said that I was the teacher who had sent him the manila envelope with the student letters. He smiled broadly and said that he was very touched by the letters. He said that he wanted to extend his appreciation to the students for their thoughtfulness. He also added that he receives many requests to visit schools, but he simply does not have the time to do that. I asked him if I could get a picture with him, and my wife stepped forward to take the photograph. We shook hands and said good-bye. I turned to Debbie and said, "Thank God the line for the bathroom was long."

When I returned home from school on the Monday after our visit to New York, the light was flashing on the phone. The message: "This is Philippe's friend, Kathy O'Donnell. Philippe would like to visit your school. He will wave the regular fee; all you need to do is provide the limo cost from his home in the Catskills to Schenectady and back." Disbelief. I called her back immediately, and it was true. We chatted about the essentials. I remember her saying that it was a very busy time for Philippe because *Man on Wire* had been nominated for an Academy Award, and he was making appearances across the country. He did, however, have an opening for us.

There is nothing like fulfilling the wildest dreams of students. When I told my classes that Philippe was coming to visit our school, they were thrilled. They even talked about rigging a rope up in the gym or my classroom to see him in action. I said that he would be addressing them, but asking him to perform on a rope was out of the question.

Two months before Philippe was to come to our school, we lost an extraordinary math teacher and school musical director because of a sudden heart attack. The school grieved and marked his life with numerous memorials. The day Philippe arrived, I escorted him to the gym where the seniors and juniors had gathered. As we walked by our school chapel, he looked at the memorial, which featured a director's chair with the name Maguire written across the back, and on the seat a calculus text and his yard stick. Philippe asked what this meant, and I told him about the school's loss.

In the gym, Philippe was at his very best. He spoke of his early years as a student and how frustrated and limited he felt in the classroom. Instead of classroom work, he would practice his magic whenever he had a free moment. He spoke about being arrested over and over in Paris because of his street tricks, including climbing lamp posts and performing on top of them. Expelled from many schools, he shared his dreams of becoming a street juggler, and especially a tightrope walker. He recounted the day when he first saw the drawing of the yet-to-be-built World Trade Center and how he drew a line between the Two Towers, while he was waiting to have his tooth repaired in a dentist's office, and how he quietly and quickly tore the illustration out of the paper and left the office without getting his tooth fixed. Using the lines of the basketball court, he showed the students how he measured out his crossing on the cable between the Two Towers - one short distance at a time. He encouraged students to live their dreams, to walk their own tightropes. "Every task," he said, "can be approached as an artistic performance, even daily living." He told them to "always strive to do their absolute best."

Among the many questions asked by the students was this one: "Do you have any regrets in your life?" Philippe said that he had no regrets, except regretting those he had loved and lost, "Just as you have felt the loss of one of your dear teachers over the past two months." As he said these words, the gym grew still for a moment. I was surprised and pleased that he had made that link. The guidance counselor told me days later that Philippe's statement had helped some students deal with the loss of Tom Maguire.

When he finished his talk, a student near me said, "To be honest, this is the first assembly I wish had never ended." We exchanged gifts. Philippe gave the school an autographed copy of his book *To Reach the Clouds*. The students presented him with a school shirt, a hat, a mug, and a key chain. He stayed for nearly an hour, chatted with the students and faculty and autographed books for the students - a number of them had brought the illustrated "The Man Who Walked Between the Towers."

Three weeks later, *Man on Wire*, directed by James Marsh and starring Philippe Petit, won the Academy Award for Best Documentary. "He won. I can't believe it," said one senior, "and he was actually here in our school."

The Classroom: Stories of Laughter, Sadness, Music, Misses and Near Misses

Laughter

On the shelf behind my classroom desk sits a small orange stuffed creature, a huge grin on its face. It was given to me in one of the faculty gift exchanges at Christmas years ago: A reminder of the importance of humor. A colleague of mine once told me that when he was a student he and his friends would make a judgment the first day of class about the teacher that stood in front of them - did the teacher smile? Did he or she have a sense of humor? That would be the measure of whether or not the class would be tolerable or not for the year. James Thurber once said that "Comedy is tragedy plus time." That truism I believe holds true for first and second year teachers who are just developing a classroom presence. In general, the more you teach the more the comic side comes into play.

My first semester as a new teacher had many rocky moments. Although I had a Master's Degree in Secondary Education, I had never done student teaching. Thus, I was trying to discover daily what worked and what didn't. One afternoon, things went badly - as I remember, most of the class had not done the reading assignment. In addition, I couldn't get them to be quiet. Suddenly, I picked up a book and slammed it on the desk and said, "All right, just shut up and sit there in silence! My voice and my red face surprised even me! For next 25 minutes or so, the class sat in silence. I would impose my glare if there was even an attempt at a whisper. The bell rang bringing more relief to me than it did to them. When they were exiting, obviously in a very different mood than when they normally left my room, I heard one of the incoming students ask what happened. "He went nuts," said one of the departing.

On another occasion, when the students did not meet my expectations, I did not slam a book, but spoke passionately, with my face flushed I am sure, about their responsibilities as students. As I finished my speech, I glared at the class. One girl who had a great sense of humor and who was sitting in the last row of the middle aisle looked at me and winked. I said, "That means you too, Anne," but her wink had already shattered my attempt to be stern.

One day, at my wit's end, I sat down in the dining room of the convent, which the Sisters of Notre Dame had generously offered to the faculty, providing us with soup, salad, and usually a choice of sandwich or casserole. I was seated directly across from a wizened little nun named Sister Brunette. She had been my financial savior many times, often on Friday afternoons. As I passed the bursar's office, she would look up at me and smile. After a few "good weekend" words exchanged, she would say, "Could you use a little help?" I would nod, and she would reach under her blotter - and take out 40 or 50 dollars and hand it to me. I always paid her back on paycheck weeks, but on the off-weeks, she gave me hope. So this day at lunch, she looked at me across the table and said, "Having a bad day, Paul?" I nodded and told her that nothing seemed to be working that morning. She cleared her throat and said, "Well, Paul, there is an old French saying, 'La vie est un sac de mensongs.'" I looked at her puzzled, and she said, "The translation is 'Life is a sack of lies.'" I almost gagged on my food in laughter. I never expected such "advice" to come from her. As I exited the dining room, I was still smiling. My afternoon went a lot better.

On the last day before Christmas vacation of my first year teaching, classes were ten minutes shorter because of an assembly. I thought I had planned enough, but with fifteen minutes left, I was done. Thank God for imaginative students. "Could we do take-offs of our teachers?" one girl asked. I was tense and didn't think it was appropriate. "Come on," another student added, "we won't be mean or anything." I breathed deeply, looked out the window in my door toward the hallway - still nervous. "Ok," I said, "but nothing mean." The boldest girl, the one who had proposed the idea, stood up and said, "I want to do you." I stepped back in fear and apprehension. She started, "Now class, I am going to play Act III, sc. 1 of *Hamlet*, which you have already read." She started to move toward an imaginary record player on my desk. Her hand mimed putting the record on, and lifting the arm with the needle. Then she paused, "But before I do, let me tell you about the time..." And she was off with an imaginary story. Then "Ok, class, let me play it... What I want you to remember...." Each time she was about to play the recording, she would pause and launch into another story or direction. Tears were pouring out of my eyes in laughter. Then she walked to the front of my desk as she was telling the last story and proceeded to walk in a pattern that she repeated over and over, while lifting and adjusting an imaginary tie. I realized for the first time that I had patterns I didn't even know about. When she was done, I led the applause with tears still rolling down my face.

In 1975, Notre Dame, where I had been teaching, merged with Bishop Gibbons, the Irish Christian Brothers' school a few blocks away. The initial jolt of awakening that I was in a different world happened the first day of orientation, when John, one of the Gibbons boys, a strapping two hundred plus pounder, entered the main office and said to one of the Brothers, "Ok, Brother Smith, I am ready for you." Brother Smith, who was young and strong, stepped forward from behind the main counter. John put up his right arm on the counter, and Brother Smith did the same from the other side. For about ten seconds, I watched in trepidation until Brother Smith with one smooth effort brought John's arm down. I breathed a sigh of relief. I wondered if I needed to go home and start lifting weights.

A month or so into the school year, I gave my first test to a senior class, a combination of essay and objective. A few days later, I returned the tests. As the students were exiting, one stopped and said, pointing to his test grade of 78, "What is this?" I said, "It's a 78." He responded, "I never got below 90 on an English test in my life." I said, "Yes, but that is a solid 78 - you can count on that grade." He looked at me and said, "I'd rather have a flimsy 90." As time passed, I realized that I had set a precedent. Students would say as they handed in their test or paper, "Now, this is solid."

We had read William Carlos Williams' poem, "Nantucket," a short lyric poem in which Williams uses specific details to evoke a definite emotional response. He doesn't tell; he shows. I asked the students as a homework assignment to write a poem about a place that reveals itself through details. I said that they didn't have to tell the reader how they felt; if the details were right, the reader would know. The following day, the students took out their poems. Standing in front of the class, I looked down at a student's paper - I could see that it was only two lines long. I said, "Walt, that is a pretty short poem." He looked up with a grin and said, "You'll never forget it." The favorite of many of the students, Walt loved to laugh and have a good time. He was also the starting guard on the basketball team and a cross country runner. While training for cross country, the students had different routes, one of which took them around the apartment complex, the Wade Lupe Towers, where my wife and I lived. The basement of the building had a laundry room, storage areas, and a bathroom. The doors to the outside were often open, and some of the runners would pop in to use the bathroom. I said to Walt, "Ok, can we hear it?" From his desk, he read the poem, "Go to Wade Lupe/ Take a poopee." The class, of course, roared, and I must admit I laughed too. Although the poem did produce laughter, I knew I would give it a check for minimal grade: translation - you turned something in.

Over twenty five years after Walt graduated, I pulled up to a red light in town and glanced over to my left. There was Walt in a truck. I waved and he did too. Then he lowered his window, and I did too. "Remember the poem," he said, smiling. I said, "Go to Wade Lupe, take a poopee." We both roared with laughter as the light turned green.

Some students are simply unpredictable, although when you think about them, you know that you should have expected what happened - or a variation of what happened. Maureen, a bright, earnest senior, had chosen to do her persuasive oral report on why women should not be forced to wear bras. In the desk right in front of Maureen sat Dan, a bright-eyed, mischievous sort. He watched her with a grin on his face. Maureen ignored all distractions and went on passionately about society's imposition of its standards on women. She cited examples of bra burning that had taken place at different campuses and among women's organizations. Her voice intensified as she built her case. Then she drew to a conclusion. Her last line, said with fervor, was, "And so, I ask you for your support." The "t" sound of the word support was barely out of her mouth when John lifted both his hands palms up right in front of her. I think she hit him with her speech as she stepped away from the podium. The class was in hysterics.

Some texts do not require pulling teeth for immediate interest. Tennessee Williams' *A Streetcar Named Desire*, for example, has such great characters, such an intense conflict, and such provocative themes. Sometimes, however, the greatest text in the world is not enough. As the class of seniors entered my room to start period 7, Anthony, a jovial and good-hearted student, passed close by me and said, "You ain't getting shit done today." The class had been a challenging one, primarily because of some intense fighting - mostly verbal - among a group of girls in the class. The battle really came down to one girl with one ally against a group of six or seven girls. The issue was over a former boyfriend of a member of the larger group being interested in the one girl. Most days, things stayed under control, but this day, the acrimony and snide comments escalated. Its competition was Scene 6 of *Streetcar*, a particularly powerful moment in the play which culminates in Blanche telling Mitch about her former husband and her role in his death. It is a stunning moment of character revelation. As we moved into the reading, a counter text had begun - in addition to the words that were being murmured, there was unbeknownst to me a notebook which had cruel and crude comments being somewhat discreetly passed around. The students reading were losing their focus, and I said at one point, "Ok, let's get serious," and "Whatever is going on, stop the nonsense." I think it was at this point that the girl who was the target of much of the vitriol discovered that she had sat on something - ink I believe. She was wearing white pants, and she stood up totally distraught. She asked if she could be excused and I let her go. I tried to restore some order, but the other girls were now in a gleeful state and were whispering to each other. I said, "Ok, that's it for today. Just sit there!" And I threw my book on the desk. I looked down at Anthony, and he shrugged his shoulders, saying non-verbally, "What did I say?" James Thurber was right. At the time, I was so angry; today, I think Anthony's

"You ain't getting shit done today" was one of the most memorable lines in my career of teaching. He knew that nothing I could do would eclipse the battle that was going to happen that day in my classroom.

One morning as second period was about to begin, the students rushed into my room on a tsunami of laughter. "You wouldn't believe what Mr. Maguire just said. It was hysterical," they screamed. Now, for Tom Maguire to say something clever or do something outrageous was par for the course. A genius, a superb math teacher, a lover of the theater, a wit - he was one extraordinary human being. A bundle of energy at about five foot five, he broke every rule that should govern a teacher's behavior in dealing with discipline problems: he pinched ears, he pulled hair, he whacked students with yardsticks, rulers, anything within his reach and made them write 100 word paragraphs after school until their arms were numb. He called them fools, and morons, and jackasses. And the students absolutely loved him. And they learned. Oh, they learned. He knew how to reach students: if one approach didn't work, he had another fifty up his sleeve.

Tom was sick of the phrase that the students used constantly, "That's what she said." He told the class one day that their use of the phrase was idiotic. "You people use it all the time - it has no meaning; it's just dumb." He went on, "You have no sense of theater, no sense of drama, no sense of timing. You're all fools." And so a month went by before the return to the phrase. According to the students in the calculus class, Tom had written a calculus problem that stretched from one end of the blackboard to the other. He said, "Ok, let's take a look at this problem." One student in the back blurted out, "That's the longest one I've ever seen." Tom turned to the class, lifted his eyebrows and in a perfectly enunciated phrase said, "That's what she said." They danced and screamed and roared, until he said, "Enough, you morons."

Sometimes students like to test the teacher's words. Since childhood I have had a fear of snakes. My mother was the principal force in establishing this fear. It had to do with the Bible and the Garden of Eden and the Devil. It also had to do with being Irish and the story of St. Patrick driving out the snakes. When my parents purchased a statue of the Virgin Mary for the back yard, my mother made my father get a hammer and chisel and remove the plaster snake that was under Mary's foot. And so snakes became one of the dark forces in my dreams. In the movies I hated the moment when the snake jumped out and threatened to bite someone - or did bite someone. I carried this burden well into my teaching career. And then I read a book called *Dream Power*, by Ann Faraday. She said that the dreamer must turn and confront whatever the dreamer fears. You need to stand and face the dark force. That seemed to make good sense to me.

A few weeks later I had a vivid dream. In front of the apartment complex where I lived, I stood face to face with a cobra. About 75 feet apart, we both wore cowboy hats, and we were both wearing holsters with two pistols. As I stared at the upright cobra, it hit me. The cobra didn't have any hands - and with that thought I drew and blew it away. And the dream worked. For a few months I did not have any dreams of snakes attacking me or surprising me. Then I made a mistake and told one of my senior classes about the amazing change in my life due to a book called *Dream Power.* I had beaten the snake fear. A few days later when I was working at my desk, I heard a voice of one of four seniors who were hiding behind my file cabinet located next to the doorway. "Heh, Mr. O'Brien," he said. I said, "What?" to the invisible person. "Here," he yelled, "catch!" And two hands threw a snake - three or four feet long - at me. I leaped out of the way - and my heart jumped a foot in my chest. "Got cha," they said, as they burst into the classroom laughing and then proceeeded to pick up the rubber snake.

Student priorities and teacher priorities often do not jive. My colleague and good friend had told me that he was fed up with doing stories like "Boys Will Be Brutes" and books like *Mrs. Mike* with his Regents level senior class. "I am going to throw some Blake at them," he said. "Why not do something that really matters to me." I responded

43

with some trepidation. "I don't know, Jeff, it may fly right over their heads." I knew Jeff, a voracious reader, had done some serious work on Blake in graduate school, and so he would be bringing a lot to the table.

He told me later about the epiphany in class. He had presented Blake's idea of innocence and experience. Then he launched into the poem "The Chimney Sweeper," by presenting the historical context of the poem. While talking about Blake, he noticed that Jessica, in the front seat to the immediate right of where he stood, was playing with three matchbox cars. He entered the first stanza of the poem talking about the narrator being sold into the slavery of chimney sweeping by his father after his mother died. He glanced down at Jessica's desk. She had two cars lined up behind each other with a space for the third car to fit. He didn't say anything to her but went on into the narrator's vision of paradise. Jessica groaned - he looked down and noticed that she was trying to park the third car between the other two - and had just bumped the front car with the third. And he went on about how easy it is when the conditions are right for people to be manipulated into doing something that will only destroy them. Some students actually seemed to be listening. Jessica groaned again. She had bumped her car again. "And so Tom awoke and rose in the dark/ and got with our bags and brushes to work," he said. He knew the poem by heart - he didn't need a text. And so he said to the class, "This poem is about the betrayal of England's young not only by their fathers," his voice rising, "by their bosses, by the Church, even God - all who tolerate such an injust system." Jessica erupted with a "Yes!" "Oh my God," he thought, "she got the idea." And then he looked down at her desk and saw the car parked neatly between the other two. Yes, she had gotten it right.

Sadness on Campus

"The day the music died" is the most significant line in Don McLean's song "American Pie." The line refers to the plane crash on February 3, 1959, which took the lives of three musicians: Richie Valens, the Big Bopper, and McLean's hero, Buddy Holly. So much promise and so much musical talent gone forever. When a student dies, sometimes suddenly, the death leaves a hole that is almost impossible to fill, especially in a relatively small high school such as Notre Dame-Bishop Gibbons.

When I think of Julio, the first thing that comes to mind is him standing in front of me after AP class the day I had passed out the research paper assignment.

I said, "Yes, Julio, what can I help you with?" He held the list of authors in his hand, "Can you give me an author who makes me think?" I looked at the list - a few students had already selected certain authors, and said, "Take a look at Flannery O'Connor, a Southern writer, who explores issues of faith in common folks. She is wickedly good and she will make you think." He said, "Ok, I will take a look at her this afternoon." The following day, he came up to me and said that he would like to do his paper on her. As I remember, the final paper was well done, but Julio's comment as he turned it in was what meant the most, "You were right. She did make me think. A lot."

Julio lived with his Mom and sister, and it seemed his father spent most of his time in South America. A bright student, Julio was accepted at a prestigious university, which required him to take a summer program to help with becoming assimilated into the university. On a Monday late in August, I was driving to Albany to pick up my older brother. We were heading south to Seaview Golf Resort, a Marriott complex a little north of Atlantic City. It would be three days of pure enjoyment all paid for by my magnanimous brother-in-law. As I started my drive, I saw Julio pass me in his grey Honda. I knew where he lived and thought I would follow him and check on how his summer program had gone, but when I glanced at my watch, I saw that I was actually running a little late. And so I drove on.

When I got home on Wednesday night, there were a number of calls I had to return, a few from one person, our dean of discipline. When I called her, she told me that Julio had committed suicide. It was hard to take in. I asked her what had happened. She said that Julio's mother, who worked a night shift as a nurse, had found him when she got home in the morning. He was in the garage on the floor with his hand near the manual garage door opener. Carbon monoxide. There seemed to be the indication that he may have changed his mind, but his body had been too poisoned by that time. He had left a note. Subsequent days and discussions revealed only that he had struggled with the summer program and that he had had some problems with his girlfriend.

I remember his classmates - all graduates now - meeting back at the school. Stunned, baffled, angry, they spoke of Julio and what he had meant to them and how they found it so hard to understand why. I wondered over and over if my following him home and chatting with him could have made a difference. It was one of those "if only" moments. Probably not, but the thought is always there. And when I think of him, I will always remember his comment about Flannery O'Connor: "She did make me think. A lot."

Danny was a gifted performer who had starred in our school musicals. Outgoing, blessed with ebullience and charisma, he was loved by both his peers and the faculty. Having graduated, he began college, but during his time there something went terribly wrong. The history of his experience is blurred in my memory, but I do recall that during Christmas time the Albany area had been experiencing a number of robberies of fast food establishments, particularly Big Dom's Subs. Watching the local evening news one night, I saw a story about a robber who had been shot and killed while trying to rob Big Dom's. It was a shocker, but I didn't think beyond that. The following day the news featured a picture from the morgue of the dead robber - distorted and swollen. His face looked unfamiliar to me. According to what I was told, his Mom had heard about the shooting, and was very apprehensive - Danny had not been around the house in some time. When she and her husband went to the morgue, they discovered that it was indeed their son.

I remember hearing the news the morning we were to leave for Boston for a post-Christmas party at my sister's. I said to my wife, "I have to go to the site of the shooting and see for myself." Because of the robberies, Big Dom's had hired a security guard who waited outside the subshop in a van. Danny, as I was told, entered the subshop with a toy gun in his pocket. He showed it and apparently asked for money. When he exited, the guard shouted at him - I don't know what Danny did - but the guard fired and hit him in the neck. He staggered down the street, around the corner of St. Vincent's Apartments, and died just past the apartment complex. When we got there the morning of our trip to Boston, I parked the car and told Debbie that I needed to do this. The temperature had been very cold, and even though the shooting had taken place a number of days earlier, I saw the vivid blood markings on the sidewalk. I followed them, imagining what it must have been like for Danny knowing that he had been seriously wounded, around the corner, past the entrance way to St. Vincent's and then to a wrought iron fence that somehow he had managed to get over. In a pile of snow on the other side was a large patch of blood. Where he died.

Such a bright star, extinguished much too early in one of life's darker traps. Regardless of all the outstanding qualitites we have, a dark pathway can eclipse everything. Bill Rago in the film *Renaissance Man* says to his class at one point, "The choices we make dictate the life we lead." This is true, but sometimes the lesson is very hard.

Jordan was the star of our basketball team. With a huge shock of red hair, he appeared to be much taller than his 6' 2", and with his great leaping ability, he sometimes seemed to be by far the tallest guy on the court. Jordan was in two of my classes, and had made a strong impression on me in both classes. In Pop Culture, he and three other students had made a thirty second commercial which bordered on the edge of inappropriate, but it was so well done and so funny that it passed the test. It was called "Manpons" - the male answer to Tampons - in the form of a traffic cone. It was hilarious. And his film team had also included some great out-takes entitled "Banana Phone." In my English class, Jordan had volunteered to play the part of Mitch in *A Streetcar Named Desire* and was playing Mitch as kind of a country bumpkin - a bit distracting but he was so good as the yokel that I let him continue with it. He was very funny.

On a Friday in November, Jordan received a notice that Bard College had awarded him a full scholarship, combining both his athletic skills and his academic success. That night he was out celebrating, and as the story was told to me, he was a passenger in a car and had been celebrating his success by lighting cherry bombs and throwing them out the window. At one point, a group of guys after hearing a cherry bomb go off gave chase. The driver of Jordan's car sped away but lost control of his car and hit a tree. Jordan died instantly.

Two memories: At the wake, the ongoing loop of Puff Daddy's "I'll Be Missing You" with the power point visual loop of Jordan's brief life. The second memory is of his desk in my classroom: first seat, third row. The first day back to class after his funeral service, a student placed five roses on that desk. For about two weeks, the roses stayed there, and then I put them in a vase with "In Memory of Jordan" written on the front and placed the vase on the mantel behind my desk. I had deliberately left one rose with a long stem. When you looked at the vase, one flower rose above the rest, like our red-haired Jordan rising for a rebound.

Rarely do students not graduate from our high school. Most of the students are quite capable, and the school goes out of its way to see that each student turns in all the work that needs to be done in order to fulfill requirements. My final for Pop Culture was a take-home. I had copied five profiles from the *New Yorker* magazine. Each student had to choose two of the five, and for each one the student had to annotate the text - required with the paper - and then write a ten page paper on the portrait presented of the artist or writer. (Who is this person? What did you learn? What were the transformational moments in this person's life? etc.) Isabel never turned the paper in, even with the pressure of graduating, and so since the final was a third of the grade, she failed the course. The school requirement is that all classes be passed.

Isabel had transferred to ND-BG two years earlier from a large, suburban high school. She was mercurial: at times, she was exuberant and involved; at other times she could go into a funk and not be productive. My most vivid memory of her in high school was an occasion in which she ran a pep rally. Her presence and command of a gym full of students was stunning. I remember saying to myself that she had a lot of gifts and one was leadership.

For two years, after she should have graduated, I would occasionally talk to Isabel and her Dad about finishing the "simple " assignment so that she could graduate. Finally, I met her at a local diner, and we had a long chat. She had been dealing with some drug issues, and she had spent some time at a rehab center. But she agreed to get the work done so that she would be a graduate. We set a time frame, she selected the two profiles she would do, and she vowed to finish them. Approximately two weeks later, she turned the assignments in. I had told her that I would treat her to lunch as a reward, and a few days later, we met at a little restaurant on Jay Street. She was in great spirits: though she had lost her license, she had purchased a new bicycle, she had a new apartment, and she was working as a waitress at a local restaurant. She spoke about her rehab period, and she felt that her life was now coming together.

As we stood on the corner by the Open Door Bookstore after our long, leisurely lunch, I looked at her and said, "Isabel, are you going to make it now?" She smiled widely and said, "Yes, I am." Eight days later, on a Saturday morning, her father found her dead in her new apartment. A party at her apartment the night before. A drug overdose. At the wake, I remember hearing one of her friends say, "We shouldn't have left her alone." In Isabel's case, the road had been reestablished, but the demons were too strong.

Shannon stood in front of the room facing Jimmy. Both held scripts, and they were reading/acting out their one-act play. I sat in the back of the room, watching and listening. Shannon read a line that went something like,

"If you don't come to the lake, I will kill myself." Then she reached into my desk, a tall desk with just one shelf for my teacher stuff, and pulled out a gun. She lifted it and pointed it at her own head. "Wait, hold it, please put that down," I said, almost falling as I tried to get out of my chair. Approaching the desk, I could see that Shannon had lowered the gun to the top of the desk, and it rested in her turned-over right hand. "Could I please have the gun, Shannon," I said reaching for it. She lifted it up and handed it to me. "It's only a pellet gun," she said, "and it's empty." I looked at the two actors and said, "I'm sorry, you simply cannot use this as a prop. You will have to use your finger if you feel that it is necessary. Shannon, can you see me after class?"

When she approached me, I told her how shocked I was that she had used a gun - a pellet gun was very dangerous - and that I couldn't let her take it with her. "Is it your gun?" I asked, and she told me that it was Andrew's, her boyfriend. I said, "Have Andrew see me at lunch." I immediately went to the Dean of Discipline, Brother Kevin, who told me that I could not allow Andrew to take the gun and that Andrew would have to call a parent or guardian to come to the school to pick it up.

When Andrew walked into my classroom during his lunch break, body slumped and the most depressed look on his face, he said, "I am sorry, Mr. O'Brien, I didn't think it would be a problem." Imagine the most introverted, shyest person you know, and Andrew was a match for that person. I did not teach him, but would often see him after school when he cleaned my classroom - he was on our work-study plan to help with the cost of tuition. To offer an apology was a courageous act for him. I told him that the basic rule is that you can't have a gun in school, and it had been a scary moment in class when Shannon surprised us all by pulling out the pistol. He apologized again. I asked him if his Mom or an adult in his family could come after school to pick the gun up. He said that his Mom worked three jobs and that there was no one else who could do it. I told him that I would drive to his house after he had gotten home from work-study and return the gun.

I had been teaching for about 30 years, and I knew the area around our school, but I had never been on Andrew's street, and though I had been through some very poor sections of our city, I did not associate such poverty with our students. I pulled up to his house - a rusted-out car up on blocks in the yard and boarded up windows in a house that hadn't seen paint in years. I was stunned. How did he afford our school, even with the work study program? To this day I reflect on what it must have looked like for neighbors to see me walking across the dirt lawn and handing Andrew a paper bag containing a gun.

About three months later, I awoke to the lead story on

the news - "Woodlawn Fire Kills Teenager." In just seconds, they identified the person as Andrew McMahon, a student at Notre Dame-Bishop Gibbons. I remember staring at the television and thinking of Andrew on the porch of his house. Because the family had been unable to pay their heating bills, they had relied on space heaters. One had malfunctioned. Andrew's mom and sister made it out; Andrew didn't. Andrew's death was a major blow to the school. I remember how much the teachers worked to console and support the students that day and the days that followed. A very sad time. I had seen first hand what some students have to deal with as they try to forge ahead with their education.

Miracles do happen - yes, that was the word used. Tommy was a junior at our school when he died on a Friday in early November. After a long battle with liver cancer and a transplant failure, Tommy succumbed. An athlete with a gentle spirit and a great smile, Tommy had played football and was a member of the basketball team. That same Friday was the first game of the basketball season, and the opponent was the previous year's Section Two champion, Albany High School. The team elected to play and wore black arm bands in tribute to Tommy.

By the end of the third quarter, all was as expected - Albany 57, Gibbons 39.

Then the fourth period began: Gibbons couldn't miss, and Albany couldn't score. As the period grew closer and closer to the end, the gym was a madhouse, frenzied beyond belief. Then with one second left, Mark Nealon launched an 18-foot jump shot from the corner. With the ball in the air, the buzzer went off - and the ball swooshed perfectly through the net. Score: Gibbons - 59, Albany 57. Gibbons had scored 20 points, and Albany had scored 0.

Coach Don Blaha said, "It was the greatest thing I have ever experienced as a player or coach. We had a tragedy here this morning, and the game was dedicated to Tom right from the start. It didn't matter if we won or lost. We just kept telling the kids we couldn't quit. And the kids dug down deep when they had to."

The clippings from that game I taped to the inside of my closet door, and over the years I have shown them to individual students as an example of what the spirit and inspiration can do.

Music:
Spirit in the Classroom

I think that shortly after I realized that a sense of humor was absolutely essential to maintaining my balance and equalibrium as a teacher, I began to see that music was an essential ingredient to tone, temperament, and spirit in the classroom. I can't think of the number of times I would put on "Staying Alive" as the students entered the classroom, especially in the morning. And inevitably, the dancing and the Travolta imitations would start. Even the most depressed student would have a hard time fighting the dancing spirit that the song evokes. Often when a big game was coming, I might start a class with the song by Dan Fogleberg, "Center Field," as a salute to a player eager to get in the game, or when I wanted to be humorous and say, "Ok, here's the word for the day, " and play "Surfin' Bird" by the Trashmen. And then there were the more formal uses of music in the classroom.

For example, in a senior elective entitled "Search," the students painted while listening to different forms of music: classical, jazz, and rock to illustrate how music affects one's emotions. It is difficult to imagine teaching for 47 years without the strong support of music.

After September 11, 2001, all of us struggled to find some solace in the darkness. When I realized that I could not go to the World Trade Center to assist in the recovery, my wife and I headed north on the Friday following the tragedy to Warrensburg where we had made reservations at the Merrill Magee House. As we entered the town, we saw signs for a candlelight vigil that would take place starting at 7 p.m. at the bandstand in the heart of the town. We checked in, had a light dinner, and then walked to the drug store across the street and bought some candles. At the grandstand, we stood listening to the town officials and the firefighters speak about the week and what had happened. We joined in singing patriotic songs and listened to the tributes. Then the Chief of the Warrensburg Fire Company took the microphone. He spoke of losing his closest friend on a battlefield in Vietnam and of how one song by Billy Ray Cyrus more than any other song spoke of what his friend's life had been and meant. "And today," he said, "the heroism of the New York firefighters and policemen brought that song once more to my mind. Listen carefully," he said, "I think you'll agree." The song he played over the microphone was Billy Ray Cyrus's "Some Gave All."

That weekend in Warrensburg inspired me to write an article for the *Daily Gazette*, the local paper. The article appeared one week later, and every year after, I would read the students the article showing how one person responded to the tragedy, and then I would conclude with the song "Some Gave All."

I was also fortunate that fall to attend a workshop at the New York State English Council's Conference entitled, "Responding to 9/11 Through Music." The presenting teacher had selected three musical artists who had spoken in their music of the tragedy: Toby Keith's "Courtesy of the Red, White, and Blue"; Alan Jackson's "Where Were You When the World Stopped Turning"; and Bruce Springsteen's "The Rising." The workshop leader had passed out the lyrics, and then he played each song, stopping after each one to look at the song for purpose, tone, imagery, and theme. It was an excellent exercise because of the sharp differences of vision in the three artists. Pop culture was speaking to all about the tragedy and calling on us to look at our country, our soul, and our vision.

For the next few years, I used this presentation in all of my senior classes on 9/11 and asked the students after some discussion to write an essay in which they compared the three songs of Keith, Jackson, and Springsteen.

Sometimes an idea comes along that focuses and aligns something that has been in your head for many years. In late 2008, a fellow teacher said to me that I needed to check out a CD called "Playing for Change." I did, and the CD and idea became part of my classroom and part of my thinking. The mind behind the idea and the execution of the idea is Mark Johnson, a producer and sound engineer, whose goal is to "inspire, connect, and bring peace to the world through music." The whole idea began when Mark, out for a walk in Santa Monica, California, heard a street performer, Roger Ridley, singing, "Stand by Me." Mark says, "I ran over to witness the rest of his performance and I have never been the same since. His voice, soul, and passion set us on a course around the world to add other musicians to his performance" (Playing for Change). Mark asked Roger if he could record him on the street, then take the song and have it performed by artists from countries around the world, who would bring their own style and interpretation to the song. And so, "Playing for Change" was born. Artists playing one song, but in their native land of Italy, Spain, Ireland, Nepal, South Africa, Israel, Portugal, etc, all beautifully edited together as if the world had joined as one.

On the jacket of his first CD entitled "Playing for Change," Mark writes, "As a human race we come together for birth, we come together for death. What brings us together in between is up to us. Stop and listen to the universal language of music and bring that positive energy with you everywhere you go."

In the classroom, I played this musical DVD more than any other single album over the last few years. I played songs from it as students entered the class, I used individual songs as classroom prayers, for example, Bob Marley's "One Love," and I would often have the DVD playing in my room after school. One afternoon, long after classes had ended, a senior stood and watched a few songs from the DVD. At one point he turned to me and said, "If we could get all the major leaders of the world together and make them watch some of these performances, the world might be in better shape."

Very few things are as personal and as meaningful to students as their choice of music - what inspires them, what brings them solace, what reflects their anger, their hatreds, their loves. In a unit on music in a senior elective entitled Popular Culture, I gave the students the following assignment. They were to come up with a list of their top ten favorite songs. Their assignment was to write a paper which began with an introduction that described the role of music in their lives; then make a list of their top ten songs, each one annotated with what made that song special. Then each student would do an oral presentation to the class, moving from ten to number one on their list. Brief comments about numbers ten to four; more discussion of the final three, with excerpts being played of each of the final three. I illustrated for them what I expected by creating my own top ten. I began with Del Shannon's "Runaway," which I explained was a song directly connected to an experience with a girlfriend, a time for me of adolescent depression. Shannon's words, "As I walk along, I wonder what went wrong" told me that I was not alone.

My number one song was "It Was a Very Good Year" by Sinatra. I spoke of the purity of Frank's voice, the complement of a full orchestra, and the idea of seeing each stage of life as being worthwhile. The conclusion is where I want to be when the days grow short, "I think of my life as vintage wine, from fine old kegs."

The students exceeded my expectations. Most of them couldn't wait to present their top ten; some were apprehensive about whether "their songs" would be appreciated by the class. It was the most positive oral presentation that I can recall ever assigning - students not only respected each other's choices, but waited eagerly to hear what the selections were going to be. Sometimes vigorous nodding when a classmate picked a song that was a mutual favorite; sometimes serious looks as they listened to music they had never heard before; sometimes good-natured laughter when a student would say, "I really like only one genre of music," and then would play ten country songs or ten hip hop tunes. Still the respect held, and the class flowed.

As an example, Sean, concluded his top ten with "Hey Jude" - the Beatles. "Hey Jude, in my opinion, is the greatest song of all time. I was probably first introduced to it in a trailor for a movie which I never saw and don't remember. Even so, I fell in love with it immediately and always remembered the closing, 'Nah nah nah nah nah nah nah

nah nah nah nah, Hey Jude." I didn't actually know the name of the song until a few years ago, but everytime I heard it, I couldn't stop listening to it. My Top Ten has been full of songs that swell into amazing closings; this one swells enough to top them all. Paul McCartney's quiet vocals and piano are slowly joined by the rest of the Beatles, and they in turn grow and grow until an entire orchestra joins in singing the three minute nah nah nah ending. This ending sends the Beatles into history and solidifies their position as the greatest band of all time." Yes, personal taste and the heart and mind of a student.

One of my favorite skits from *Saturday Night Live* that I used at least once a year, often to get the class started, was a duet of Frank Sinatra (played by Joe Piscopo) and Stevie Wonder (played by Eddie Murphy). The premise is that Frank wants to create tunes that the "young people will enjoy" and has decided to collaborate with Stevie Wonder. The interplay between the two characters is hilarious as they decide to sing a song, "Ebony and Ivory," that was recorded by, according to Frank, "the Beatle kid that looks like a broad." Blending Frank's rough edges but bullheaded determination with Stevie's ability to go with the flow results in the classic tune. The skit ends with Stevie looking at Frank and saying, "You are white" and Frank countering with, "You are black - and who cares!" Humor making its point through music ("Ebony and Ivory" SNL).

Occasionally, as the students were entering the class-room, I would as the song says, "Hit 'em with a little Ghetto Gospel," with Elton John and Tupac Shakur. The song pulls no punches about the state of the world, "But am I less holy 'cuz I chose to puff a blunt/ And drink a beer with my homies/ Before we find world peace we gotta find peace/ And end the war in the streets my Ghetto Gospel." The heart of the song's plea is in these words, 'There's no need for you to fear me/If you take your time to hear me/Maybe you can learn to cheer me/ it ain't about black white/ Cuz we're human I hope we see the light before it's ruined/ My Ghetto Gospel." ("Ghetto Gospel" CD). The two artists' collaboration is a message in itself.

Over the last 25 years or so, I had gathered a pretty good collection of rap and hip hop artists. For the most part I kept many of them in my CD collection in school, and I would use some for specific reasons; for example, the sheer fun of "Rapper's Delight," a song guaranteed to lift the spirits and a song many students know by heart, was a perfect opening on a slow Monday morning. DMX's "The Prayer" actually worked very well as an occasional opening prayer in my classroom. I would put on Eminem's "Lose Yourself" or Tupac's "Thug Heaven" just because I liked them, often after school; sometimes between classes. But I think the chief benefit of having a broad range of CDs, including rap and hip hop, is that it opened up discussion to new types of music and voices that needed to be heard. After school, students would sometimes drift in to listen to one of my CDs or have me listen to their songs. Then we would share ideas about music and art and life.

Another SNL star's song also became a staple in my classroom. Early in the year - usually in the first ten days or so, I would play the musical close of Dana Carvey's first HBO Special. The segment I would show ran about 8-10 minutes and portrayed Carvey satirizing different types of music and artists, but the end was his signature touch. Putting down the guitar, he ran over to the piano and started making a point about how trite some lyrics are, and he illustrated it beautifully and hysterically with a song, "The Lady I Know." The song builds to his great little "Choppin' Broccoli" bit that is pure nonsensical fun. It is so well done that even the most depressed and burdened students are laughing at the end.

Anyone who is down in spirit can see the power of music by looking at the film *Almost Famous* and the sequence with the Stillwater band after a disastrous, truncated concert. The band and their girlfriends are riding on the bus, and the mood is total depression and glumness. Then the music of Elton John's "Tiny Dancer" comes on, and in two minutes you see the miracle take place, like stagnant water into sparkling wine. As the song's words are heard, "Hold me closer tiny dancer," you see the band members and those riding on the bus start to join in, and even Russell, the band's leader, who has been lower than a snake's belly, joins in and the scene culminates with the entire bus singing euphorically the words to "Tiny Dancer."

I had seen Jonathan Demme's film *Heart of Gold*, a 2006 documentary of Neil Young performing his album "Prairie Wind." I loved the movie and told a good friend about it, Brother Joseph Fragala. He seemed very interested, and so he and I and another teacher went to the theater to see it. He loved the movie and bought the CD. One song in particular he played over and over, "When God Made Me." The song spoke to the heart of Brother Joe, the idea that permeated his being: that there is room for all, that multiple voices are out there and that they should be heard, that the answer to so many problems is not exclusiveness, but inclusiveness, and that we are given gifts that we must use. Brother died in the summer after seeing this film. The following year at the baculaureate Mass, one other teacher and I sang "When God Made Me" in honor of Brother Joe.

Misses and Near Misses

The fall musical at the school that year was "You're a Good Man, Charlie Brown," a production filled with loveable characters and all the fun troubles of Charlie's world. On the night of the Friday production, a heavy rain fell outside, offering a kind of contrapuntal effect to the spirited songs of the play. Given the weather, it was a good audience, and they enjoyed the production. Outside in the darkness, rain would become the least of the worries for a number of the people attending the play. In the parking lot, there were approximately eighteen cars that had tires cut during the production. Seventeen had one tire cut; one car, a teacher at the school, had three tires cut. In the rain, people expressed shock, anger, and frustration. And then, as often happens in the darkest hours, light came in the form of five or six seniors led by Bill, who masterfully orchestrated, with each driver's approval, the changing of the tires. Those who had suffered the damage waited in the school, while the seniors worked in the rain. The only difficulty was the teacher's car with the three cut tires, but the students managed to secure two more donuts from other cars that did not have damage. So the teacher drove home that night with three donuts on his car. The seniors who had taken over had changed the mood of the evening dramatically.

But two questions were foremost: Who had done this damage and why? A few of us speculated on the one car with the three tires cut. Had the others been cut to camouflage the main target, the teacher's car? Ralph, the English teacher, was a bright and clever man who taught high school as if it were college. He was rigorous and demanding and presented challenging texts. He loved verbal exchanges with the students and wouldn't hesitate to be sarcastic. The sarcasm worked better with the bright students; the average students sometimes resented it and felt a kind of mockery.

About two weeks after the tire cutting, Bobby and Vince, two students I had taught the previous year and related well with, entered my room after school and closed the door. Both wearing long leather coats, they approached my desk. "Do you have a few minutes?" Bobby asked. I said, "Sure, guys, what's up." They remained standing. Again Bobby, "We need to talk about something." I said "That's fine - go ahead." Sometimes life has a way of intruding at the wrong time. Over the public address system, "Would Mr. O'Brien please report to the main office immediately!" I started toward the door. "Listen," I said, "I don't think it is anything that will keep me, so stay here. I'll be right back."

As I descended the stairs, I felt the urgency of returning to that room. I reached the office to discover that my older brother had called, and I needed to call him back.

I took the phone and called immediately to find out from him that the family just needed to meet to talk about my mother's will. We agreed on a date.

I knew before I got back to the room that they wouldn't be there. Courage sometimes fades quickly. When I asked Bobby and Vince the following day when I could see them again, they just said, "Ahh, we're good."

Both were students in Ralph's senior English class, and neither one - I was told when I inquired further - had a fondness for their teacher. That day I believe in my heart and soul that they were going to tell me what happened on the rainy night. The opportunity was lost, and no one ever really discovered who and why.

I became reaquainted with Danielle on Facebook. I had missed her the first time. Few things are more troubling to a teacher than a former student telling him that she was in your class, and she didn't really exist. "You don't even remember me, do you?" I tried to recall and recover her presence in my classroom. "Didn't you sit in a back seat about in the center of the room?" I asked. "No," she smiled, realizing clearly that her point had been made. "I sat towards the back in the first row." To make matters worse she added, "And you also taught me English sophomore year."

She had me although I tried to make a case that the senior class she was in was a very difficult one for me. I had found a number of the students hard to teach and difficult to manage. Still there had been a student in the class - and how many others over the years - who had felt that she didn't exist in her teacher's mind.

Danielle had gone on to college for a psychology degree and had earned her master's in the field of social work. She is now a very effective case worker for the department of social services, a difficult and challenging world. She told me - and I had a vague recollection of a student doing this but never linked it to her - that she had spent her junior year in high school studying in Bolivia, thanks to the efforts of her mother in finding the program. If I had been alert and more aware of each student, Danielle could have become a source of so much helpful information about studying in other countries and living at a young age away from home.

I had neglected her in class, and I wondered over the years how many others I might have missed on my radar. "You don't even remember me, do you?" A difficult question for anyone, and especially for a teacher.

I had followed Richie's career at our high school because he was destined to be one of our school's success stories. Entering Gibbons with a couple of scholarships, Richie, blessed with strong home values and charisma, had been at the top of his class at a local Catholic grade school. And in his first year at the high school, he proved true to his promise, ending up with the best average in his class. As a sophomore, I taught Richie and saw early that he had real insight into the literature we were reading and an ease with expressing his ideas, but as the year progressed, his relationships and interests seemed to shift, and he descended academically into the middle of his class. The guidance counselor stepped in and tried to decipher what Richie's issues were. As a junior, he barely passed a number of Regents' classes. His choice of friends and the interests of his friends, I was told, had sharply shifted his priorities. Not only had he fallen academically, but his social relationships were now narrow, and he had become defiant and belligerent towards adults.

I was determined in my senior English class to give Richie my best shot, firing up my most enthusiastic self for Sherlock Holmes, Willy Loman, and Blanche DuBois, but I could see that he was not really present to me. A few times, I sought him out to engage him in ideas about the texts and sometimes just gently inquire about how he was doing. In his emerging character, he had become harder and colder. He kept things to himself, and I couldn't find a way to break through. The first marking period ended with Richie failing three classes, including mine. Because of the failures and because he had violated a number of school rules, Richie was given a warning that unless he changed his ways, he would have to leave the school.

Roughly three weeks later while teaching, I heard from my classroom the loud slamming of a locker. I opened my door, and there was Richie dumping stuff from his locker onto the floor. "Richie," I said, "What are you doing?" Seething he said, "I'm outta here." He turned and walked directly toward me - he had failed my class - and I wasn't sure in his anger what he'd do. Would he try to punch me? He took a deep breath, extended his hand and said, "Thank you, you were always fair to me." I was stunned and looked him in the eye, "Richie, I hope you make it."

Dwayne entered my class well into the fall semester. When he arrived from guidance about ten minutes late, I welcomed him, pointed to a seat, and said, "Dwayne, we are about half way through *To Kill a Mockingbird*. I will fill you in later." Dwayne looked at me and said, "I ain't reading that shit." Both the class and I were stunned. I couldn't believe that he had been that rude the first day of his arrival from another school and that he dismissed the text so crudely. "Dwayne, see me after class," I said and went on with the lesson.

"I'm telling you," he said defiantly, "I ain't reading that shit." Rather than ask him for his commentary on a text that was "beneath" him, I took another route.

"How about *The Adventures of Huckleberry Finn*," a text the class had already completed. "Nope, I know about that one!" I figured one more try before I walked him down to guidance for further discussion, "What about *The Old Man and the Sea*," I asked. He looked at me, "What's that about?" I said, "It's about an old man who sets out to catch a fish, goes out too far, and gets in trouble." He looked at me, "Ahhhh, ok."

About three weeks later in math class, Tom Maguire, known far and wide for his unorthodox approaches to discipline, attempted to pull his ear when he noticed that Dwayne did not have his homework done. Dwyne jumped up and shoved Tom, a diminutive fellow, so hard he went flying against the wall. Another student, burly and strong, leaped in behind Dwayne and grabbed him firmly and held him. Then he was escorted out of the room and expelled that day. I found out shortly after, that in the school he had come from he had tried to exit a classroom by throwing a chair through a window. I was not sure I would have wanted to know that detail ahead of time.

But there was one brief, shining moment in Dwayne's short stay. In my class I had the students write a poem in which they found beauty in the most mundane of things - an exercise that Kenneth Koch uses. Dwayne wrote: The dazzling light/ of the sun/ on the broken glass/ made it look/ like it was having/ all the fun."

Keith's paper was once again not on time. Exasperated, I looked at him. "Keith, see me after class." Once the class had exited, I got into my little rant, and like most teachers, once we get going, we have to do our thing. Keith, tall and bespeckled, stood off to my right. "Look, Keith, this is getting ridiculous. This is the fourth time in a row that you have not handed your paper in on time. And you, Keith, are the only one who didn't turn it in. What makes you so special when all the others get it done. It's not as if I am asking you to write an epic poem. Tell me, Keith, why it isn't in on time!"

He looked at the floor and then sighed deeply. "Look," now he was glaring at me, "you have absolutely no idea what my life is like and what I go through each day. Every single day it takes me more than an hour to put on deodorant under each arm - that's two hours. Everytime I use my computer at home, I have to clean it thoroughly and here at school I can't touch the keyboards of these computers at all - only if I can have plastic put over the keys so that I am protected from the person ahead of me." He went on for another two minutes - impassioned, flushed, almost in a rage. And the key phrase that permeated it all was, "YOU have NO IDEA what I go through." When he was done, I looked at him and said, "I'm sorry, Keith. I will make every effort to be understanding and fair to you in the future. But you, given all of the factors that weigh on your every action, have to make every effort possible to complete the task." We stared at each other, and almost simultaneously we extended our hands and shook.

About five years later, my wife and I were dining in a local restaurant, and who should approach our table but Keith. We greeted each other and then he took our order. Later, when he was dropping our bill, he said, "I guess you probably noticed that I am much better. I got some help and now I am for the most part in good shape. Look, I am even a waiter in a public restaurant and am constantly handling dishes of other people." I said, "That's great, Keith," and I left the restaurant with a good feeling that sometimes one can overcome.

Heroes and
Inspirational Forces

A Newer World

In the early 1960's Robert Kennedy had come into my life and grew dramatically for me in the next few years. As I began to teach in 1967, he was one of the principal forces shaping the way I saw the world.

On June 4, 1968, I stayed up late watching the reports on the returns from the California Presidential Primary. After a tumultuous and exhausting campaign, Robert Kennedy appeared to be the winner. Having to teach the next day, I went to bed with the feeling that there was hope for America in this charismatic, contradictory, inspirational figure. By morning, my world and the world of all those who saw hope in Robert Kennedy had been tragically diminished.

I knew very little about Robert Kennedy in my formative years. I knew that he was part of a bright and influential family. Of course, Irish households in general saw his brother John as an heroic figure and a game changer. I remember being called in by my parents from the woodshed - our game center - to watch the Presidential Debates of 1959: John Kennedy vs. Richard Nixon. I remember clearly with all the bias built into an Irish household how handsome and articulate Kennedy seemed against the darker, tortured figure of Nixon - a beacon of hope versus a flickering lantern. In our eyes, Kennedy was the clear cut winner in the debates, and we would have disputed totally the analysis of political pundits that the debates were actually very, very close. Theodore White's *The Making of the President 1960*, a book I later devoured, made me see much more clearly how close the debates and the Presidential race had been.

Not being a political person by nature, I did not engage in late night college tavern discussions about how the Kennedys were doing as leaders, although I was aware that Robert had been a crucial figure in the Cuban Missile Crisis and a strong voice to the President on domestic issues.

Robert Kennedy's life and the world's took a dramatic turn on Nov. 22, 1963. I was walking up North Avenue in New Rochelle heading to my American Literature class with Dr. Peter Chetta, when cars starting pulling over. One man who pulled up near me had his window open, and I could see that he was listening intently to his radio. I asked, "Did something major happen?" Looking directly at his radio, he said, "The President's been shot." In class, Dr. Chetta moved slowly to the front of the room, turned and said, "Gentlemen, given what has just happened, there is no way I can conduct class. Go do what you need to do." I am still amazed to this day that about twenty minutes later about 100 young men gathered in the quad near the ginkgo tree and prayed the rosary. It was a prayer I knew well.

The images of the Kennedy funeral are forever locked in the minds of those who were alive at the time: The stoic face of his wife, Jacqueline, the salute of his son, John, as his father's body passed by, the riderless horse, Blackjack, who carried a saddle with boots turned backwards in the stirrups, and the one constant image, the presence of Robert Kennedy at Jacqueline's side, both consumed by grief, both plumbing depths of strength to carry on.

At the 1964 Democratic Convention, filled with political manuevering, Kennedy stood before the delegates on the fourth day of the Convention and received a twenty-two minute round of applause. Lyndon Johnson, the Democratic choice for President, had told the convention organizers that the ceremony planned for day one would not take place until day 4 of the Convention. Johnson, according to many political pundits, feared a ground-swell of support for Kennedy that would move him into the position as his running mate; and LBJ, whose relationship with the Kennedys was rocky to say the least, feared and disliked Robert Kennedy most of all. On day 4, one could see why the fear was legitimate. The outpouring of emotion was overwhelming on the floor, as Robert

Kennedy stood at the podium waiting to give his tribute to his brother. Tears rolled down my eyes.

The speech was relatively short, citing some of the accomplishments of his brother, but two moments especially stood out for me. "I realize that as individuals we can't just look back, that we must look forward. When I think of President Kennedy, I think of what Shakespeare said in *Romeo and Juliet*: 'When he shall die, take him and cut him out into stars, and he shall make the face of heaven so fine that all the world will be in love with night and pay no worship to the garish sun'" (Kennedy, R. Speech). And then at the very end of the speech, Robert mentioned that his brother often quoted Robert Frost and that the following lines applied to the President himself, "The woods are lovely, dark and deep, but I have promises to keep and miles to go before I sleep."

Robert Kennedy had become foregrounded in my life, not as a maneuvering politician, which he was, but as a character as rich as those created by Shakespeare: Someone who had experienced tragedy and someone who was growing into an understanding of tragedy's full potential.

As Kennedy's campaign for President was beginning to gather steam, the world was rocked with another assassination. On April 4, 1968, Martin Luther King was shot and killed while standing on the balcony outside his room in Memphis, Tennesssee. The night before, King had uttered prophetic words in his sermon at the Mason Temple in Memphis, Tennessee. "Like anyone, I would like to live a long life. Longevity has its place. But I'm not concerned about that now. I just want to do God's will. And He's allowed me to go up to the mountain. And I've looked over. And I've seen the Promised Land. I may not get there with you. But I want you to know tonight, that we, as a people, will get to the promised land! And so I'm happy tonight. I'm not worried about anything. I'm not fearing any man! Mine eyes have seen the glory of the coming of the Lord!" (King Speech). Profoundly prophetic.

For many, the people whom King had spoken for and represented, the poor and down-trodden, the assassination was the tipping point. Violence exploded in many cities, especially in the slums of Baltimore, Chicago, Washington, D.C., and Detroit. Kennedy was in a plane heading for Indianapolis when he heard that King had been assassinated. Against the advice of a number of his supporters and the city police, he, upon arrival in the city, went immediately to the rally site that had been arranged for him in a poor section of the city. On the back of a flatbed truck, he began, "I have bad news for you, for all of our fellow citizens, and people who love justice all over the world, and that is that Martin Luther King was shot and killed tonight." Gasps, screams, and cries poured forth from the crowd, and then Kennedy continued. He spoke about

King's dedication to peace and justice. He spoke about the temption for bitterness and the desire for revenge on the part of black people. He said that we could move in the direction of "greater polarization or we could make an effort as King did - to choose, instead of violence, understanding, compassion, and love." He spoke of his own loss and spoke of his struggle to understand, to get beyond the dark times. And then he quoted one of his favorite poets, Aeschylus: 'Even in our sleep, pain which cannot forget falls drop by drop upon the heart, until in our own despair, against our will, comes wisdom through the awful grace of God'" (Kennedy R. Speech 1968).

His closing words were "And let's dedicate ourselves to what the Greeks wrote so many years ago: to tame the savageness of man and make gentle the life of this world. Let us dedicate ourselves to that, and say a prayer for our country and for our world" (Kennedy R. Speech 1968).

Two months later, Robert Kennedy was assassinated.

In many ways, the funeral for Robert was more painful. I had felt an identification with him that I had never felt with his brother John. For me President Kennedy had remained a hero who had opened new worlds - romantically captured in the word Camelot. Robert, perhaps because of my own growth in maturity and insight, was someone I could identify with, someone with obvious flaws, someone who clearly bit his pencils, but also someone who had seemed to find a connection with the common man, the downtrodden, the poor, the minorities. Ted Kennedy, in the close of his eulogy, touched the heart of what Robert Kennedy was to so many: "My brother need not be idealized, or enlarged in death beyond what he was in life; to be remembered as a good and decent man, who saw wrong and tried to right it, saw suffering and tried to heal it, saw war and tried to stop it. Those of us who loved him and who take him to his rest today pray that what he was to us and what he wished for others will someday come to pass for all the world. As he said many times, in many parts of this nation, to those he touched and who sought to touch him: 'Some men see things as they are and say why. I dream things that never were and say why not'" (Kennedy T Speech).

I had often read Jack Newfield's column in the "Village Voice," a paper I had started to read in fits and starts in college. Newfield was a strong liberal and someone who had come to see in Kennedy a beacon for the future. His book, *Robert Kennedy, A Memoir*, was published in 1969. The jacket shows Kennedy's face, touseled hair, serious expression, a finger crossing his lips, eyes looking at both the reader and slightly to the reader's left, but the eyes - to me edged with sadness - reflecting most of all, pensiveness. The book ends on an ominous note with the author speaking of this recent period of history: "We are the first generation that learned from experience, in our innocent twenties, that things were not really getting better, that we shall not overcome. We felt, by the time we reached thirty, that we had already glimpsed the most compassionate leaders our nation could produce, and they had all been assassinated. And from this time forward, things would get worse: our best political leaders were part of memory now, not hope. The stone was at the bottom of the hill and we were alone" (Newfield 304).

Newfield's book became a permanent part of my classroom, whether in one of my bookcases or resting against the chalk board with Bobbie looking out at the classroom. A postcard commemorating him and including the passage from Aeschylus was taped under the clock near the entranceway to the classroom. The book disappeared from my room sometime in 2009-10. Someone had borrowed it, but it never came back to me.

One poem discussed in class usually following the reading of Homer's *Odyssey* was Alfred Lord Tennyson's "Ulysses." Part of the reason for my desire to do this poem was its link to RFK, in addition to the fact that the text showed how rich the evolution of the figure of Odysseus over the ages has been. Tennyson presents a figure of the old King as someone who still seeks to explore and know more - to set out on the sea in search of new ventures and new discoveries. "Tho' much is taken, much abides; and tho/ we are not now that strength which in old days/

moved earth and heaven, that which we are, we are;/ One equal temper of heroic hearts,/ Made weak by time and fate, but strong in will/ To strive, to seek, to find, and not to yield" (Tennyson 560). Inspirational words that close Tennyson's poem, but the line that Robert Kennedy spoke more than any other line in his campaign was one that appears a few lines before the closing of the poem: "Come, my friends,/ 'Tis not too late to seek a newer world." I cannot think of any more inspiring words for Robert himself, almost shattered by the loss of his brother, than those words from Tennyson.

A student from the graduating class of 2010 gave me a large framed poster promoting Robert Kennedy for President, 1968. The poster was issued by Students for Kennedy, Princeton University. In the sketch Kennedy looks to his left, dress shirt open, tie loose, and at the bottom of the picture, the words, "Seek a Newer World."

Courage, Grace, and Magic

In the last thirty years of my teaching, my classroom was always graced with a picture or a quotation from three African-American athletes: Jackie Robinson, Arthur Ashe, and Muhammad Ali. In the case of Robinson, I created an assignment flowing out of the Ken Burns' documentary "Baseball." The other two figures were there because they, along with Robinson, had informed my thinking about our culture and our character. Each man had faced great adversity and had overcome incredible odds to achieve his goals. I wanted their image to be a reminder to my students of what can be done: Robinson with his guts and courage; Ashe with his quiet dignity on the tennis court and beyond; Ali with his firey poetry and politics. They were of a particular race, but they rose to heights that spoke to all of us. I call them Courage, Grace, and Magic.

Jackie Robinson: An ideal summer night in Cooperstown. A perfect night to take advantage of the instructor's words at our Advanced Placement workshop in the little town known best for its Hall of Fame.. "For those of you looking for something to do tonight, there is a lecture at the Cooper History Museum on Jackie Robinson by Professor Arnold Rampersad of Princeton." After a dinner in town, I drove the short distance to the museum and parked the car at the far end of the lot - there were a lot of people coming to his lecture I thought. The arrow for an event featuring the lecture by Rampersad pointed in the direction behind the museum. In just a few moments, I saw an enormous white tent and a few people strolling around outside the tent; most of the people I could see were seated at tables inside. Walking down the hill, I felt like a total outsider. I was dressed in loafers, summer shorts, and a polo shirt; everyone there was dressed in tuxedos and fancy summer dresses. I kept walking and approached the main entrance to the tent.

A tall, stiff-looking man dressed in tails approached me. "Can I help you?"

"I was hoping to hear Professor Rampersad's talk on Jackie Robinson," I said, with a touch of pleading, after I had detected his disdain.

"This is a major fund-raising event for the museum," he said in a superior tone.

"Is it possible that I could sit off to the side, kind of out of sight to just hear the speech?"

He looked exasperated, but then glanced back to his left where there were a few chairs and unused tables just past the coffee urns. "All right," he said, "sit in one of those chairs but stay over there."

I was audacious, "Is it possible to have a coffee?"

"Absolutely not," he said. "That coffee is for the guests who paid for this evening."

He escorted me to the out of the way location and then pointed at a chair.

I sat down and in a way had the last say because in my front pocket, I carried a small tape recorder all set to go. He never saw the recorder, and I taped the entire talk.

I think I was drawn to the Dodgers and Jackie Robinson in the 50's because the Yankees dominated the baseball world and seemed invincible. I remember as a young boy listening to the radio as the Yankees seemed to win game after game, against Boston, Chicago, Detroit, whoever they played. I remember my father groaning at another Yankee win - and so it seemed inevitable that when the Yankees were in the World Series, I would cheer for the underdog. In the 50's, that often was the Brooklyn Dodgers.

My first hero with the Dodgers was Duke Snider, the center fielder. I remember listening to the Dodgers on the radio and feeling so excited when the "Duke of Flatbush" hit a home run. My brother and I owned a Roy Campanella catcher's mitt and a Gil Hodges' first basement mitt. I remember Carl Furillo's great throws from right field to nail runners; I remember Pee Wee Reese and Jim Gilliam in the infield. On the mound, Carl Erskine, Don Newcombe, Johnny Podres, and the brilliant Sandy Koufax. And, of course, Jackie Robinson. I even remember seeing on our black and white Halicrafter's TV Jackie sliding under Yogi Berra's glove. Stealing home? Yes, Robinson did it.

In 1957, it was over. The Dodgers moved to Los Angeles, and, for many Dodger fans, it marked the end of an allegiance. Still one Dodger light grew brighter over time. I began to see much more clearly Jackie Robinson's role in baseball history and in the history of this country. In 1994, Ken Burns' wonderful documentary "Baseball" cast a brilliant beam on the Negro leagues and on Robinson's heroic role in baseball. Each year in my senior elective "Pop Culture," I showed "The National Pastime - the 6th Inning," which covered the emergence of black players into baseball, led by Jackie Robinson. Before watching, I gave the students an essay question: In what sense could one consider Jackie Robinson a hero?

Burns' technique, as most know by now, is to use still photographs, a few video clips, and commentators who knew the principals and/or the world they were part of. When Branch Rickey had decided to bring a black player to the white Dodgers, Red Barber, the sports' announcer who had been born in Mississsippi and raised in the South, spoke of how difficult it was for him to adjust to the presence of a black man in baseball and how much Robinson changed him over time. "Robinson," Barber says, "matured me." Barber recalled Branch Rickey's potent question to

Robinson before signing him: against all the bigotry Robinson would face, Rickey asked, "Do you have the guts not to fight back: for three years, you will not fight back" (Sixth Inning). After some thought, Robinson agreed that he would not fight back.

There are certain moments that stand out in films that you hope also ring true with your students. There are many in Burns' film, but three stand out especially for me. Historian John Thorn's thought: "I can think of no man having a more difficult road ahead of him than Jackie Robinson did in 1947 and no one walking that road more valiantly and more proficiently. I would say that Jackie Robinson is my great hero as a baseball player, and he is my great hero as an American. He is an individual who shaped the crowd" (Sixth Inning). The second moment: On the evening of April 15, 1947, a Jewish family gathered for Seder in Brooklyn. "Why is this night different from all other nights?" a young Jewish boy asked his father. And before his father could reply, the boy answered, "Because a black man is playing in the Major Leagues" (Sixth Inning). The final moment for me and the thought that closes the segment on Jackie Robinson is from conservative columnist George Will. "The most important black man in American history is Martin Luther King. A close second, I would argue, is Jackie Robinson, who came before Martin Luther King and began the consciousness-raising of whites and blacks that resulted in Martin Luther King's career. The heroism of Jackie Robinson ... to play with his intensity under the pressure he felt on and off the field from racism; to do all that under all that pressure is not just one of the great achievements in the annals of sports but one of the most heroic dramas anywhere, anytime" (Sixth Inning).

If any students were to have looked closely at me during any of these three moments, they would have seen me wiping tears from my face.

On the wall to the right of the door of my classroom, I had placed at eye level the book jacket of Arthur Ashe's memoir, *Days of Grace* featuring a facial profile of a thoughtful Ashe. Underneath the jacket is an editorial entitled "Arthur Ashe, Model Champion." It begins, "The rise of Arthur Ashe in tennis, crowned by his Wimbledon victory in 1975, took on the stature of a fable. He was a black man in a sport that seemed a metaphor for racism - a sport played by white people in white clothes at white country clubs - and for a time he was the best there was. He was also a rare champion who believed that personal success imposes broad responsibilites to humanity." The editorial concludes with, "Mr. Ashe did not waste his fame; he used it to leave a mark on the social canvas of his time. For this, he remains a model champion" (Arthur Ashe).

Over the years in which Arthur's picture and the editorial graced my wall, I never made any explicit comments about him or his contributions, but he was a presence. Every so often, a student would stop and read the editorial or ask about Ashe - who he was and why he was important to me.

Arthur and I were contemporaries and though I never played tennis, except for a few fun attempts, I followed the big tournaments on television and watched as his career developed. I remember how tall and slender he appeared and how fluid and poised he was on the court. He won the U.S. Open the first year I started teaching, and he defeated the heavily favored Jimmy Connors in the 1975 Wimbledon the summer I got married.

Of course I was stunned when he suffered his first heart attack in 1979 and then underwent quadruple-bypass surgery and soon retired from the game. Then, he had his second bypass surgery in 1983, after which he received a blood transfusion, blood that was tainted, blood that would eventually cause Ashe to have full-blown AIDS. This discovery was not made until 1988 when Arthur underwent brain surgery. The amazing thing is that for the next four years he was able to keep the public from knowing his medical condition.

During these years, in addition to learning all he could about the disease of AIDS and responding as well as he was able to the best medical advice, Arthur continued to work tirelessly helping South Africa move from its apartheid state to one of integration. In Nelson Mandela, Arthur found a leader who led him to a deeper understanding of resistance. In his memoir, Ashe writes, "Mandela's example leads us to ask certain questions, on which I believe our future may depend. Can we African Americans emerge from the prison house of our history with true dignity, as he did - that is, with a determination to remain free but also without bitterness or any other compromise in our moral principles? Can we prevent our outrage at the wrongs we have suffered in America from destroying our spirit, from depriving us of the high moral ground we once held? Can we avoid the temptation to sink utterly into despair, cynicism, and violence, and thus become abject prisoners of our past?" (124-125).

When Ashe was interviewed by *People* magazine about how he was coping with AIDS, he was asked rhetorically if this disease was the heaviest burden he had ever had to carry. His response took the reporter by surprise. "You're not going to believe this, but being black is the greatest burden I've had to bear." He went on in his memoir to say to the reader, "My disease is the result of biological factors over which we, thus far, have had no control. Racism, however, is entirely made by people, and therefore it hurts and inconveniences infinitely more" (126-27).

Stature in society did not protect one from racism. It didn't matter that Ashe was not "a welfare recipient trapped in some 'blighted housing project' but rather "a former Wimbledon champion whose home was in the "wealthiest district in Manhattan." The sadness was still there.

He had grown up in Virginia under segregation of all black and white schools, riding in the back of the bus, not being allowed to apply to the University of Virginia, but even when he began to make a name for himself in the world of tennis, racism was still palpable, just more subtle. By this time too, he had become "a master at the game that all African Americans must learn if they wish to preserve their sanity: how to live with reasonable freedom and dignity and yet also avoid insult, disappointment, and conflict rooted in racism (Memoir 138).

What made Arthur Ashe an exception to much of mainstream thinking was his firm belief that success was based on one's commitment and effort; he was vehemently opposed to the concept of "You owe me," and the strategy of black power to take back a world through exclusion and violence. Ashe had the more encompassing vision: "My potential is more than can be expressed within the bounds of my race or ethnic identity. My humanity, in common with all of God's children, gives the greatest flight to the full range of my possibilities. If I had one wish, I would ask that all Americans could see themselves that way, past the barbed-wire fences of race and color. We are the weaker for these divisions, and the stronger when we transcend them" (167).

I was 10 years old when boxing first sent adrenline racing through my body. At a church square dance at a local hall, the dance committee had arranged to have a television set up to show the heavyweight championship fight between champion Rocky Marciano and former champion Jersey Joe Walcott, whom Marciano had defeated the previous year in a dramatic come-from-behind one punch knockout in the thirteenth round. I am not sure exactly how my allegiance to Marciano had started, but I was a big fan. The church goers, mostly the men, had squeezed in near the television, and I remember I had a hard time seeing through the crowd. And then it was over - a first-round knockout.

I followed Marciano until he announced his retirement in 1956, the only heavyweight in history to go undefeated in his professional career. Then my allegiance switched to a young black fighter who seemed unusually soft-spoken and gentle - Floyd Patterson. After becoming the youngest World Heavyweight Champion in history when he defeated Archie Moore in November of 1956, Patterson drove my blood pressure to heights unknown in his three fights against Ingemar Johansson. After the shocking first fight in which Johansson knocked Patterson down seven times before the referee stopped the fight, I was more on edge than I had ever been as the rematch approached. The night of the fight, I could barely catch my breath - my body swaying and contorting as I listened to the fight on the radio. In the fifth round, Patterson knocked Johansson out - and I felt a catharsis beyond any I ever felt in my life. I collapsed back onto my bed - I was so proud of Patterson. In their third and final fight, Patterson won by a knock-out in the sixth round. I was a wreck again as each fighter seemed to dominate at moments until Patterson finally asserted himself.

The darkest hour, however, was yet to come - in the form of the menacing and mob-connected Sonny Liston. Again I was a wreck before the first Liston-Patterson fight in September of 1962. It was over in the first round, the third fastest knockout in boxing history. Patterson was so devastated by the loss that he left the arena that night wearing a fake beard and dark glasses. The rematch, about one year later, had the same result. I think it was right before the fight that I borrowed a cigarette from a friend to relax myself - and then smoked on and off for the next thirteen years. Though he managed to win more fights, Patterson was never the same again. Now Liston, appearing invincible, was the champion without any apparent conquerors on the horizon.

And then Cassius Clay appeared. The first time he registered on my radar was in the Summer Olympics in 1960 when he won the Light Heavyweight Championship. Like a young god, handsome and dazzling, Clay seemed to bring to boxing a whole new approach. Dance, stick, move, jab - a whirlwind of action - confusing, disheartening, and wearing down the opponent. And Clay loved to play with words, often in short bursts of verse belittling his opponent and often calling the outcome of the fight.

Turning professional, Clay quickly moved up the heavyweight ladder, and, in February of 1964, Clay fought Sonny Liston for the championship. A seven to one underdog, Clay was in a frenzied state prior to the fight referring to Liston at the weigh-in as a "big ugly bear." Clay said that he would "float like a butterfly and sting like a bee," and "Your eyes can't hit what your eyes can't see" (Mee 180). His pulse rate was off the charts, and most people predicted an easy win for Liston.

Wrong!! Despite a fifth round in which Clay fought nearly blind as the result of ointment on Liston's gloves that got into his eyes, Clay, with his speed and footwork, eluded Liston and kept connecting with his own punches. When Liston did not come out for the seventh, Clay was the World Champion and screamed to the reporters, "I shook up the world. I told you - I am the Greatest" (Mee

193). In a controversial rematch, Clay - now Mohammad Ali - knocked out Liston in the first round. Despite the controversary of the punch that took Liston out, the evil force - I say evil because of Liston's reputation of associating with gangsters and the mob - had been conquered and in my boxing mythology a new hero had taken over.

But my hero's life soon became complicated and murky. After a few more successful defenses of his heavyweight title, including a victory over a much overwhelmed and outgunned Floyd Patterson, he faced his biggest challenge, the United States government. Having joined the Nation of Islam in 1964 and chosen the name of Muhammad Ali, he had been called to report to the Houston Draft Board in April, 1967. Uttering the line, "I ain't got no quarrel with them Vietcong," (Bingham and Wallace 124) Ali refused to be inducted into the army, making his appeal on the grounds of conscientious objection - his Muslim faith did not allow him to fight this war. In the epilogue to his book *King of the World*, David Remnick cites poet and civil rights activist Sonia Sanchez, "This was still a time when hardly any well-known people were resisting the draft. It was a war that was disproportionately killing young black brothers, and here was this beautiful, funny, poetical young man standing up and saying no! Imagine it for a moment! The heavyweight champion, a magical man, taking his fight out of the ring and into the arena of politics, and standing firm. The message that sent!" (290). (Two months after Ali's call to report to the Houston draft board, I got a notice to report to the draft board in Troy. The principal of Notre Dame High School wrote a letter to the draft board, and I was deferred.)

He had taken his stand against the war, but the U.S Department of Justice ruled against him, and he was found guilty of refusing induction into the military. Even though he was sentenced to five years in prison and given the maximum fine of ten thousand dollars, the legal battles continued and eventually the Supreme Court in June of 1971 vindicated Ali on the grounds of being a conscientious objector.

When Ali was asked if he wanted to take legal action to recover damages from those who had helped to shape his fate, he responded with "the same dignity he had maintained through his seven years as a national pariah. 'No. They only did what they thought was right at the time. I did what I thought was right. That was all. I can't condemn them for doing what they think was right'" (Bingham and Wallace 249).

For over three years, Muhammad Ali, stripped of his title, did not fight. But the years when he was at the peak of his fighting skills were not lost. His long-time ringside doctor, Ferdie Pacheco, in his book *Muhammad Ali, A View from the Corner*, says, "Forced to rely on his own initiative and intelligence, shorn of the 'support' systems of a super-star, Ali matured into manhood" (87).

And then he returned to boxing in October of 1970 after the boxing association lifted a suspension that had been in effect for three and a half years. Among the fights that ensued were brutal battles against Joe Frazier and, for me the most memorable of all, the "Rumble in the Jungle" in Kinshasa, Zaire.

Sonny Liston had been dark and menacing; reigning heavyweight champion George Foreman was young, powerful, and seemingly invincible. Ali had taken Frazer and Ken Norton into two complete fights and split with each fighter; Foreman had knocked out both Norton and Frazer in the early rounds. The destruction of Frazer with Howard Cosell's voice screaming, "Frazier is down, Frazier is down" sent fear through my veins about what Foreman would do to Ali.

Orchestrated by the charismatic and ruthless Don King, the fight took place in Zaire, Africa, on October 30, 1974. The fight was a thriller and a cliffhanger. Foreman roared out like a freight train and Ali began his quick movement and dance, but he was firing back shots. By the second round, Ali stopped his dancing and began his psychological destruction of Foreman. Resting against the ropes, Ali let Foreman launch his powerful blows into his body, leaning far back to avoid wild haymakers to the head.

Any punch of Foreman's that landed directly to Ali's head could have ended the fight. His corner berated Ali to get off the ropes, but he stayed there and screamed at George, "They told me you could punch." Ali had worked feverishly over the previous six months to prepare his mid-section for the Foreman storm. His stomach was like granite.

As Foreman began to tire, Ali began to throw punches off the ropes, staggering Foreman on a few occasions, and then in the eighth round it ended with Ali, after a series of punches, dropping Foreman with a beautiful straight right to Foreman's face. The fight was over. Ali had done it with strategy and sheer will. Ali's ring physician, Doctor Ferdie Pacheo, spoke about Ali's convoy moving through the jungle in the monsoon rain that had burst after the fight. "As we got into the deep jungle, we started to see natives coming out to the road, carrying their children and covering them with palm fronds or corrugated tin sheets. All they wanted to do was to see Muhammad Ali pass by. Just see him. All the way to N'Zele, the quiet natives lined the way, in order to someday tell their children that once, on a rain-swept morning, they had seen pass by: The Greatest!" (133).

Controversial and charismatic, inspirational and exasperating, noble and mean-spirited, Muhammad Ali was both simple and complex. But time is the true measure of a man - and Muhammad Ali undoubtedly proved his worth. From a brash young upstart in the boxing world to an amazing boxer, Ali's growth turned toward the magnanimity that was always in his heart. After retiring from boxing in 1981, Ali directed his heart and mind to helping the world. As an ambassador of peace, he traveled to Lebanon, Afghanistan, Iraq, Cuba, and, upon Nelson Mandela's release from prison, South Africa. He has served the poor around the world by promoting causes that alleviate hunger, often personally engaging in the feeding of those in need in Indonesia, Mexico, and Morocco. Kofi Annan, Secretary General of the United Nations, recognized Ali as the "United Nations Messenger of Peace," and in 2005, Ali was awarded the Presidential Medal of Freedom.

Muhammad was a man of my time who played a role in my thinking and in my life. He was a great athlete and also a man who continued to grow and mature as a human being. His magic lit the world.

Meeting a Hero

The moment that lingered in my mind and still remains long after I finished reading Dick Cavett's *Talk Show* is his account of spending a few days with John Wayne, when Wayne was filming *The Shootist,* his last picture. While Cavett was in Hollywood preparing for a prime-time special, *Dick Cavett's Backlot U.S.A.,* he had been tipped off that John Wayne was "shooting over on Western Street," and so, since Wayne was one person of fame and legend that Cavett had not interviewed or met, he immediately went to the set of *The Shootist.* What followed were three glorious days for Cavett.

When he arrived on set, Cavett, while waiting for the Duke to shoot a scene, heard him humming a familiar tune from a Noel Coward play and began to hum along with Wayne. What followed after eye contact and a shared smile was a delightful conversation about their mutual love of Noel Coward. After Wayne said that he had read most of Coward's plays and then cited some lines from a play, Cavett almost reached for the smelling salts. It was one astounding first meeting.

What followed were two more thrilling days hanging out with Wayne on the set of the film. He had a chance to see the shooting of the famous scene in which Jimmy Stewart, playing Wayne's doctor in the film, tells Wayne that, "You have cancer." Wayne himself was dying with cancer at this time, and so the line had a special power. Cavett got to sit on Dollar, Wayne's horse, and take a short ride. "His back was so broad that my painfully separated legs stuck out closer to horizontal than to the customary vertical" (264). On his last day, Wayne agreed to be in Cavett's special. Asking if the camera was rolling, Wayne took the hand mike and said, "Hi, this is John Wayne interviewing Dick Cavett" (264).

About to depart, Cavett expressed his gratitude to Wayne for letting him be a part of his world for a few days, and though he said he "felt kind of foolish," he asked Wayne for an autographed photo. Wayne agreed, got ahold of one, signed it, and put it in an envelope. On the freeway, Cavett remembered the picture. He pulled over and took it out of the envelope. On the photo were the words "To Dick Cavett from John Wayne." That was more than enough for Cavett, but below those words were written these words: "We should have started sooner."

The chapter and the book ends with these words: "You bet I cried" (265).

Meeting My Hero

Kathryn, my niece, put down the phone and turned to me. "It may not happen, Uncle Paul. Martha just told me that she has to go into the City because a good friend is very ill." I put the paper down on the table and said, "Oh well, nothing we can do about that." Inside I felt disappointed, and so, I assumed, did my niece. After all, she and Martha had orchestrated the whole thing.

Roughly a year and a half earlier, Kathryn had engaged Martha in a conversation about this meeting. Martha, Dick Cavett's wife, had been in my niece's framing shop in Montauk with a large painting. At one point, my niece mentioned that her Uncle Paul (me) thought the world of her husband. She told Martha that I had read his books, watched his television show faithfully, spoke about him often in class, and had seen Dick both on Broadway and in Williamstown's summer theater. Martha, after listening to Kathryn's account, told her that the next time I visited she would set up a meeting so that I could have a nice chat with her husband.

And so the time had come. My niece called me two weeks before the date and told me what I would do. In this case, I loved her direct approach. I was to take the train or drive down to Montauk on a Friday. Dinner with her father and her on Friday night, and then on Saturday while the three of us were attending the Montauk Histori-cal Society Annual Celebration, she and I would slip out and head over to Cavett's home. That Saturday morning she had gotten Martha's call.

On Sunday morning, about 11, Martha, who had returned from the city, called Kathryn and said that we could come over about 3 in the afternoon. Kathryn told me at that point that Dick really knew nothing about the visit except that she was coming over to look at some old frames that Martha wanted replaced. I would simply be her uncle who was down for a visit going for a ride with her. Kathryn wanted it low-key because Dick rarely received guests and preferred the quiet and solitude of his home, Tick Hall, originally a Stanford White house that had burned to the ground in 1997. Thanks to the tenaciousness and will of Carrie Nye, Dick's first wife, now deceased, Tick Hall had been rebuilt to mirror almost exactly the original house.

First, a little dog came bounding down the front stairs, followed by Martha. After a brief introduction, Martha chased after the dog, shouting to us, "Go right in and call out - 'Dick.'" We entered the house, and Dick appeared from a room adjacent to the main sitting room we were in. "Dick, this is my Uncle Paul." He looked at me and with that Cavett smile asked, "Are you a real uncle or just some-one they call uncle?" We both laughed as Kathryn said, "He is my real uncle."

Martha reentered the house and asked if I would like coffee. I said yes, with cream and sugar. She must have had a pot ready, because she returned within a minute or two with the coffee. "Come with me, Kathryn, I have to show you those frames," she said, and the two women disappeared.

And so I sat down across from the man who had been a wonderful source of entertainment and learning in the years when I was just beginning to teach and well into my maturing years as a teacher. So many amazing guests: Groucho Marx, Norman Mailer, Woody Allen, Janis Joplin, Bette Davis, Mel Brooks, Orson Welles, Muhammad Ali, Fred Astaire, Lester Maddox, Walter Cronkite, Jonathan Miller, Daniel Ellsberg, William Buckley, John Lennon, Janet Flanner, Gore Vidal, John Updike, Helen Hayes, Julie Andrews, Tennessee Williams, Bobby Fischer, Marlon Brando, Richard Burton, Katherine Hepburn, and so many more. Politics, sports, music, theater, writing, journalism, law - he covered the gamut with his guests. Every show brought food for the mind and for my classes.

I began our conversation by telling him that he had saved me emotionally at the end of my teaching career. He said something brief like, "Oh, how's that?" And I told him that I had heard a radio show sometime prior called "Person, Place, and Thing," in which each guest was asked to talk about the person, place, and thing he valued highly in his life. Cavett was the very first guest on the show. His responses had been Groucho Marx, the Sand Hills of Nebraska, and the German Lugar. And so, I told him, with the end of my 47 year teaching career coming to a close, I struggled with how I would handle the last few days. And then it hit me: I would have the students write an essay in which they selected the person, place, and thing that were of great significance to them. With a minimum of 250 words for each of the three, I told them that they would have to present one of the three to the class. And so the last two days of my teaching career were spent listening to students speak of the person, place, or thing they valued highly. When I was done recounting the end, Dick said, "Well, I'm glad I could help."

And then we were off. I had a thousand questions ready, but the conversation just flowed. I don't remember a single long pause. I do think I asked him early in the conversation what he was presently reading, and he told me he was about half way through John Laehr's biography of Tennnessee Williams. I was taken back when he said that he was struck by Laehr's occasional misuse of a word. I knew Cavett was a word maven and had even feared he might catch me on a misuse of a word or a mispronunciation. The reference to the book reminded him of the afternoon Tennessee Williams came in from the porch at that very house - well the original one - and told Dick that he had been thinking - he was no one to feed greedy egos - that Dick's wife, the actress Carrie Nye, had given the best performance of Blanche Dubois he had ever seen. I told Dick that I had seen a few pictures of him in an Andy Warhol exhibit a month earlier at the Ogunquit Art Museum in Perkins Cove. This led Dick to comment on the fact that he could never get Warhol to say more than two words to any question he ever asked.

The little dog came wandering through at one point, and we chatted about the dog for a minute, which led me to ask Dick if he had ever read Billy Collins' poem, "The Revenant," a sardonic and humorous poem about a dog that despised his master. When he said that he hadn't, I pulled it up on my cell phone and passed it to him. He read it and laughed a number of times. I suggested that to get its full effect, he might want to Google the poem with Collins reading it.

At a few moments in the conversation, he did what I do more and more often - remind the other person with a word or a phrase that I want to pick up another thread when one line of thinking is over. I was actually pleased when he corrected me about a quotation from a New Year's Eve guest, Hermione Gingold. I recalled that when he asked her if she was ever bombed in London during World War II, she had said, "I was bombed during the whole war." He said, "That's not exactly what she said, 'Bombed most of the war' were her words." This told me that the man still had great powers of specific recall.

When Martha and Kathryn appeared in the room again, an hour and a half had flown by. We had our picture taken together, and then we said good-bye. Kathryn told me that Martha had really orchestrated the whole thing, that Dick rarely saw people in the house, and that this had been pretty special. I told my niece that it was a beautiful collaboration for without her initial conversation with Martha, I would never have had the opportunity. As a final thought, I was reminded of something Dick said about Jack Parr. "Make it a conversation," Parr said to Cavett, and that was the best advice he had ever gotten about how to run his talk show. I can attest personally to the fact that my time with him was a conversation, one of the most relaxed I have ever had. Thank you, Kathryn and Martha and Dick.

Voices That Excelled:
A Student, An Alum, and A Teacher

A Rose in the Cement

Late one October afternoon, I was driving in one of the poorer, crime-ridden sections of Albany on my way to pick up my wife who was working at Higher Education Services Corporation. Listening to the radio and gazing at the people on the street, I was stunned to see the maroon and gold uniform of one of our students. It was the incongruity of Omar being in the center of a fair amount of questionable street activity that stunned me. Yet he walked in both a relaxed way and with a purpose. I felt both proud of him and in a strange way a little embarrassed about the world he had to traverse. My eyes would be opened further not too long after when a local television station profiled Omar in a segment called "A Rose in the Cement."

Focusing on students who make a difference, a reporter had spent time with Omar to see more clearly his world. One of seven children with a single parent, Omar lived in a very poor section of Albany. His mother worked extra jobs to see that Omar had the chance to go to Notre Dame-Bishop Gibbons High School located in Schenectady. Encouraged by his YMCA basketball coach, who saw in Omar a drive and a gift, Omar had become an outstanding leader at the Y, instructing other young people on the right roads. Speaking about his own demons, however, Omar shared how hard it had been for him to control his own temper - as a younger boy, he was always ready to fight someone. He spoke about his street friends and the temptations they created for him. Many of them had already had run-ins with the police, and Omar knew that unless he kept his priorities in the forefront of his mind he too could end up in jail. He said that he wanted to become a rose in the cement, someone who lives in a harsh world but manages to excel with his gifts and then help to change the world for others.

I did not teach Omar until senior year, when I was once again reminded that teaching is reciprocal - a give and take, learning from each other. The story was "Sonny's Blues" by James Baldwin, a tale of two brothers, one a successful math teacher; the other, a failure - a jazz musician but a heroin addict. The story is really about the narrator, the math teacher, coming into an awareness of his brother and his brother's suffering. My strategy often with stories that run a bit long is to read them aloud together in class, asking for student volunteers. Each student reads a page or so and then I thank the student and move to another volunteer. In these transitions, I check to see that everyone is comprehending the story.

Omar was the first volunteer. When he started, I sensed that he was immediately locked into the story. His intensity, his rhythm, his clarity with each word - the more he read, the more the story rose from the page. In a way "Sonny's Blues" seemed to be his story, and I realized in my gut that Omar had experienced many of the emotions Baldwin chose to reveal in this tale. The class settled in, and we listened together as the narrator and his brother rose up in intense conflict, and heard Sonny's words: "It's terrible sometimes, inside, that's what's the trouble. You walk these streets, black and funky and cold, and there's not really a living ass to talk to, and there's nothing shaking, and there's no way of getting it out - that storm inside. You can't talk it and you can't make love with it, and when you finally try to get with it and play it, you realize nobody's listening. So you've got to listen. You got to find a way to listen" (Baldwin 43).

It was a story about listening we knew now, and Omar was our conduit to Sonny's world. Well into the story Sonny begs his brother to come to the nightclub where he had played before. And so the narrator agrees to go. When it comes time for Sonny to play, the song becomes Sonny's, and as the narrator listens to his brother play, he understands for the first time Sonny's passion and Sonny's life: In the music, the narrator, "heard what Sonny had gone through and would continue to come through until he came to rest in earth. He had made it his: that lone line, of which we knew only Mama and Daddy. And he was giving it back, as everything must be given back, so that, passing through death, it can live forever....And I was yet aware that this was only a moment, that the world waited outside, as hungry as a tiger, and that trouble stretched above us, longer than the sky. Then it was over" (Baldwin 47). The narrator has a drink sent to the bandstand for his brother. Just before Sonny starts to play again, "He sipped from it and looked toward me and nodded. Then he put it back on top of the piano. For me, then, as they began to play again, it glowed and shook above my brother's head like the very cup of trembling" (47).

Close to two full days of reading, all by one student. It was a tour de force. Discussion followed and lots of ideas flowed especially about the final picture presented of Sonny, his fate, and his future. Most agree that the story was as much the story of the successful brother who came to see and hear and understand his younger brother for the first time in his life. By the end of the story, the narrator knew the meaning of Sonny's blues. And we all could see more clearly.

Omar stood out again in an assignment directly linked to Tim O'Brien's novel *The Things They Carried*, a memoir-like narrative of his experiences in Vietnam. In the title story of the book, O'Brien presents a richly detailed catalogue of what the soldiers carried in the jungle of Vietnam, from their clothes and equipment to their poise, their dignity, their pain, and their memories. "They carried all they could bear, and then some, including a silent awe for the terrible power of the things they carried" (O'Brien 9). But before the reading, I would ask what the students carried to school each day. Inevitably the initial responses would be things like book bags, lunches, cell phones, notebook, pens, but then someone might say something like apprehension or hope - and then discussion would evolve into how much each person actually carries with them each day - from their parents' desires and wishes to the weight of their personal relationships to fears about the present and the future and on and on. And so it was a neat transition to ask them to write about the things they carry, with the additional bonus that the essay might be material for their required college essay, or a writing sample that could be submitted to colleges. The results were for the most part honest, clear, and compelling pieces of writing. Here is Omar's "The Things I Carry."

"We all carry many things throughout our lives. Some things we carry for a short period of time, and some things we carry for the rest of our lives. We all carry things that are unique to us.

I carry my bag filled with pencils, pens, notebooks, textbooks, and all the necessities of school life. I also carry the love, joy, pain, and grievances of those dear to me. I carry the memory of my grandfather and my uncle. I carry the pain of poverty and the burden of being a victim of circumstance. I carry the dreams of my brother while he is away, and my mother's dream of wealth. I carry my family's ticket out of the struggle.

I also carry my dreams of success and happiness. I carry the hope of freeing my neighborhood from drugs and violence and prostitution. I carry the dream of giving the children of the ghetto a chance to spread their wings and fly. I carry with me the hope that one day we may realize the diversity in people and appreciate them for that. I carry with me Dr. Martin Luther King's dream of harmony.

I carry heavy baggage. I carry my past filled with days without electricity and living in hotels. I carry the burden of trying to break the cycle of inner city youth destined for failure. I carry the inner city youth destined for success. As I carry all of this, one question arises: how do I do it? By carrying the one thing I can't do without, I can do it. That one thing is God. With Jesus in my heart, my bag is a whole lot lighter."

ND-BG Alum Extraordinaire

Flashback eleven years: In response to a phone call from the development director at Notre Dame-Bishop Gibbons, Doctor Brian Hickey responded, "I can't give the school a lot of money, but I can give it my time." From that moment, Doc Hickey has given ND-BG three or four days each spring, inspiring the students with talks on everything from the physics of bicycling to his understanding of civil rights in the South to the secrets of success in college. Blessed with the gift to motivate and inspire, Doc Hickey's finest quality is his unceasing generosity.

A professor of Exercise Science at Florida A & M and adjunct professor of Health Science at Tallahassee Community College, Doc is committed to his students and their education, encouraging them always to be the best students they can be. His own commitment to athletics serves him well in the classroom. A seven-time member of the US National Team in Duathlon and Track and Field, a twenty-nine time National Champion in Masters Track and Field, Doc has also competed in the 2004 Olympic Cycling Trials and is a former American record holder in the Masters Track 4 x 800 m Relay. His first love is his wife Rachel, but his teaching and his bike are a close second.

He remembers the forces that shaped him. He speaks with glowing pride of his parents Fred and Terry Hickey who have been tremendous supports on his journey. He talks with fervor and animation about his years in graduate school at Syracuse University, where he learned what research is all about. He speaks with special fondness of Notre Dame-Bishop Gibbons, from which he graduated in 1986. He speaks passionately about how the school shaped him morally and intellectually, and recalls with special joy the night in 2008 when he was inducted into the Notre Dame-Bishop Gibbons Hall of Fame. And so when his last grades are turned in for the spring semester at Florida A & M and TCC, Doc heads north to spend a few days at his alma mater, ND-BG.

With his shaved head, eight ear-rings, and totally engaging smile, Doc takes over a room, exuding electricity and hope. His language is charged with his own idioms, metaphors, and phrases. He misses no one: to the student with his arm in the sling - "How's my boy with the injured wing?" To the student who sits alone in the back of the room, "How's my friend doing back there?" To the students desperately seeking direction, he regales them with stories that illuminate the pathway. He has visited as many as six classes in one day at ND-BG, moving through English, Morality, Marriage, Physics, Spanish, and History. By the end of the day, he is ready for his favorite restaurant food in the area, the Squire Fire Wings at the City Squire Pub. (He hopes the new ownership will keep the recipe.) His mind is charged with ways to help the school. Two and a half years ago, he suggested to the development director that he would ride his bicycle 3000 miles to raise scholarship money for ND-BG. The riding would be a virtual trip across America, though he would be riding primarily in Florida. Shortly after that discussion, the first Tour de Gibbons began with the announcement on the Gibbons home page and Facebook page. The agreement was that he would ride for $1 a mile. By late spring as Doc finished his 3000 miles, the donations went over $3000 dollars. The following year, the ride was repeated and donations went over $3500.

In the spring of 2015, Doc varied his approach dramatically and did a one-day bike ride of 140 miles from Syracuse University to ND-BG, to once again raise money for needy students who could not afford to attend ND-BG without significant financial aid. He chose Syracuse as a starting point because he had spent two years there earning his master's, running track, and serving as an academic advisor to the lacrosse team. And during that time, he found that the University was an ideal place for him to learn and train. Syracuse and ND-BG were the two schools that meant the most to him on his academic journey, thus the ride.

I was privileged to be part of this journey along with ND-BG Development Director Christine Baseel. On Wednesday, May 20, I met Christine at 10:45 p.m. at Notre Dame-Bishop Gibbons, and in the Gibbons van, we drove to Doc Hickey's parents' home in Duanesburg where we met him and loaded all the necessities for the journey, including two bikes. Arriving at 'Cuse about 2 in the morning, Christine and I were treated to a tour of some of Doc's old haunts when he was a student there: his apartment, the Varsity Restaurant - "Greatest wings ever," the Manley Field House, where he wore a groove in the indoor track. A few tosses and catches by Doc of the lacrosse ball against a wall at Manley - and we were off. We followed him on country roads in the dark to provide illumination, and then in the daylight we went ahead and waited for him at designated stops. The van served as an oasis for him, a place for a snack, a few humorous exchanges, a change of clothes. At one point we had to double back after Doc called us to say that the section of road we had already passed through in the van was closed to bicycles, thus requiring the creation of an alternate route. It was on this return that Christine and I narrowly missed getting hit by a guy who had run a red light. We tried to sleep a bit: I got about 15 minutes in the back of the van; Christine got 30 minutes. And Doc rode on. We needed at one point to double back for an equipment adjustment. The plan to stop for a quick burger at Jumpin' Jacks in the town of Scotia was scratched because time was growing short. Doc's father, a retired New York State trooper, joined him near the end, and together they rode down Albany Street, the entire Gibbons student body cheering them on, and then into the driveway of the school with the song "Believe in It" from Candlebox celebrating his return home.

In the 60's, the Beach Boys had a hit song, "Be True to Your School." I can think of no one who better represents loyalty to a school than Brian Hickey.

The front of Room 6 - home base.

Tucker riding the wave.

Amazing feats.

Laughter and Triumph.

Memory of Jordan.

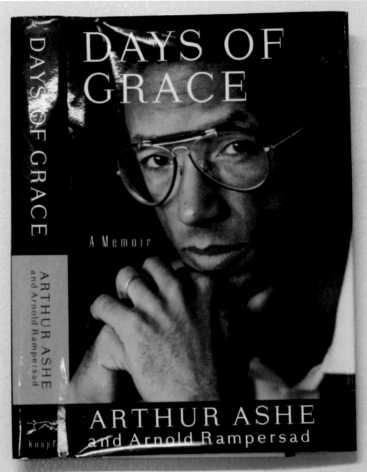

Arthur Ashe, Model Champion

The rise of Arthur Ashe in tennis, crowned by his Wimbledon victory in 1975, took on the stature of a fable. He was a black man in a sport that seemed a metaphor for racism — a sport played by white people in white clothes at white country clubs — and for a time he was the best there was. He was also a rare champion who believed that personal success imposes broad responsibilities to humanity.

Mr. Ashe's life was linked to two of the great social scourges of his day: racism and AIDS, the disease that led to his death last weekend. He confronted them head on — driven, until the end, by the unselfish and unswerving conviction that he was duty bound to ease the lives of others who were similarly afflicted.

In 1970 Mr. Ashe began a public campaign against apartheid, seeking a visa to play in the South African open. Three years later he won that fight and became the first black man ever to reach the final of the open. His appearance inspired young South African blacks, among them the writer and former tennis player Mark Mathabane. In his memoir, "Kaffir Boy," Mr. Mathabane wrote that the more he learned about Mr. Ashe the more he dreamed of freedom:

"What if I too were someday to attain the same fame and fortune as Arthur Ashe?" Mr. Mathabane wrote. "Would whites respect me as they did him? Would I be as free as he?" That dream came true when Mr. Mathabane won a tennis scholarship and immigrated to America.

Mr. Ashe took his crusade to America's inner cities as well, where he established tennis clinics and preached tennis discipline and provided hope to the young people who most needed it.

He contracted AIDS through a transfusion of tainted blood during heart-bypass surgery a decade ago. He learned of his infection in 1988, but did not disclose it until last April, after USA Today told him it planned to publish an article about his illness. After his public admission, Mr. Ashe campaigned vigorously on behalf of AIDS sufferers and started a foundation to combat the disease.

Mr. Ashe did not waste his fame; he used it to leave a mark on the social canvas of his time. For this, he remains a model champion.

Arthur Ashe.

Mentor and Coach Herb Crossman with Omar Trimino.

With Doc Hickey.

Early years with Cavett.

"Though this be madness
Yet there's method in it"

The Legendary Tom Maguire.

It all comes together

Thomas Joseph Maguire: Teacher Extraordinaire

On the way into the gymnasium of our high school, where the funeral Mass was to be celebrated, I was still in control. As one of the pallbearers for my friend and colleague Tom Maguire, I felt a great sense of loss but also a need for control. Entering the packed gymnasium, we paused in the back. Two seniors who had starred as the leads in our fall musical "Man of La Mancha" a few years prior stepped to the mike in the front of the gym. When "The Impossible Dream" began, I could feel my body start to quiver and the tears begin to fall - I remember holding the casket with my right hand and reaching in my coat for kleenex with my left. No one loved theater more, no one loved working on our school musical more than Tom Maguire, and no song could have been a better fit at that moment than "The Impossible Dream."

My job after helping to position the casket in the front of the gym was to give the opening reflection on Tom. I knew that I needed to steel myself, not an easy task because I am an emotional person, especially on the occasion of the loss of a loved one.

I began.

*Welcome to all who knew and cared for Tom Maguire.
Today we celebrate this Mass to commemorate him.*

*In a waterfall of words, the tributes to Tom have poured
in over the last few days. From those who were fortunate
enough to be his colleagues, from those who were blessed
to have had him in the classroom, from those who knew
him as a friend, and even from those who had only heard
of him. As Tom's long-time friend, Dominic Pannone, said
on the web-site, 'Tom was an original, one of a kind, truly.'*

*I would like to offer a few words today about what made
him an original. First, he was blessed with a wonderful
mind, analytical and incisive. Robert Wood, our valedicto-
rian of 2005, said in his graduation speech that Mr. Maguire was probably the 'closest person to a genius' he 'would
ever meet.' His brilliance was like a powerful magnet drawing out the thinking and reasoning powers of others. On one
of our many summer trips to Shakespeare and Company in
Lenox, my wife Deborah said that she had been reading a
book by Stephen Hawking and that the topic of infinite distance between two points had come up. 'I just can't grasp
what he is saying,' she said. 'Let me try to explain,' Tom said.
And when he was done with his two minute explanation,
she said, 'Tom, I understand it now.'*

*Second, he was blessed with the gift of compassion,
not always obvious but there in copious amounts. It was
apparent at times of struggle and loss among his friends,*

but especially evident in his eagerness to work with those students who were struggling to find their way academically, or trying to learn a new dance step for the musical.

And permeating everything he did was his brilliant wit and comic vision of the world. He kept all of his students on the edge - they never knew when he would turn to them, with a glint in his eye, and make them see what it was like to perform on Maguire's stage. As one graduate said, 'He could more than match wits with the brightest of us.' Or as Tom would say, 'It's all a matter of timing. You've got to pick the right moment.'

Finally, in one word - energy. Road Runner? Energizer Bunny? Not even close. Whether regaling our lunchroom faculty with stories that had people crying with laughter into their food, or turning to Miss Licata in the back seat of our car at 2:30 in the morning after a long Yankee game - Debbie asleep in the front seat, me driving with my eyes squinting wondering if I could focus enough to get us home - and saying, 'Now look, Toots, you have to stop taking crap from these kids. Here's what you need to do,' the energy never waned. And maybe the best example: as I would leave school, exhausted - in need of an afternoon nap at home, I would pass his classroom door. His room was blazing with activity: kids working on math problems at the board, five or six students surrounding his desk listening to him explain a formula, three or four kids writing his famous punishment paragraph for their inappropriate behavior, usually someone doing a chin-up on his door - Tom leaping up, banging his yardstick on the desk, and yelling a name - 'Listen, you, get to work now or else!!' I'd pause in the doorway, smile and leave school wondering, 'My God, how does he do it?'

More and more over the last few days, I have been thinking about the relationship between Tom's two loves: teaching and theater. I can imagine no one in the last 50 years experiencing more theater than Tom - his close friend Melba can attest to that by the playbills that filled his basement. He saw it all - from the irreverent and bawdy to the thoughtful and tragic, from high school gyms to the Globe Theater in London. And this love for the theater was inextricably interwoven with his passion for teaching. For he brought all the insights into the human heart from his theater experiences to his own stage in the front of his classroom. The more he saw, the larger and wider the experiences, the better the teacher he became. He was right when he said, 'I don't need posters. I am the whole show.'

This fall the seniors had the opportunity to see the film Man on Wire, the story of the stunning accomplishment of the tightrope walker Philippe Petit, who walked between the two towers of the World Trade Center. An audacious and awesome example of what we can do when we have the tenacity to follow our dream to fulfillment. Tom's walk had taken him from his boyhood at St. John's Grade School in the south end of Albany to Cardinal McCloskey High School, then to Siena College and onto RPI, and finally to Notre Dame-Bishop Gibbons. And though his first year of teaching was difficult and discouraging, he gathered himself together, rose above all obstacles, and went on to become, over 42 years, more of a teacher, I would guess, that he ever dreamed. He became a star on the most significant stage of life. Yes, he was a teacher, one of a kind."

It is December 30, 2008, and I am standing at the Championship game of the Kirwan Cup Basketball Tournament - one minute to go. Gibbons is trailing Mohonasen High School by two points, and we are bringing the ball down the court, when Christine Baseel, colleague and friend, hands me her cell phone that reads simply, "Tom Maguire died this afternoon." I stare at it in disbelief and turn to Christine and say, "Is there any truth to this? Where did it come from?" She tells me, and then I say, "Do we really know for certain?" I am climbing down from the bleachers - Gibbons does not score and Mohonasen has the ball with a few seconds left. Christine is frantically trying to get back to the person who texted the message. I reach the parking lot without confirmation and start driving home when my cell phone rings. It is Deborah, my wife, who sadly informs me that Tom Maguire is in fact dead. We commiserate briefly, and then I call Christine, who suggests that we meet at the Blue Ribbon Diner and let any students who need to deal with Tom's loss come and be with us. I agree, but when we reach the Blue, the diner is closing, and as an alternative, we choose the local Applebee's and send out messages to key people that we will gather there. Within thirty minutes, Applebee's is crowded with students and teachers who knew and loved Tom Maguire.

That afternoon before he died, I had gathered with Tom and seven other teachers and staff at the Italian Center for lunch. Tom complained about not being able to get warm that day, even when he turned the shower to its hottest and had the car heater cranked up to its maximum. An ominous sign. The luncheon was enjoyable and filled with good stories and laughter - a hallmark of wherever Tom would be. One moment haunts one of the people who was present that day. Barbara O'Brien, former business manager of the school, had been talking to Tom and had told him that he needed to start collecting on his social security. "I turned to him" she recalls, "and said, 'Tom, do it now, you don't know how long you have here." Within three hours, Tom was dead of a heart attack. Another person at the luncheon said, "Tom had his tickets for *Billy Eliot* for the Saturday coming up and was so looking forward to it!" An expert tap dancer himself, Tom Maguire would have been in heaven at *Billy Eliot.*

Imagine a person of inexhaustible energy in whatever he did.

Imagine a person with a lightning mind as quick as Hamlet's.

Imagine a person who broke every proper disciplinary procedure known to teachers and thrived in his iconoclastic world.

Imagine a person who could see five plays in one weekend in New York City and teach Calculus on Monday.

Imagine a person who was so present in the theater in his front row seat that even leading actors would play to him.

Imagine a person who stayed after school for hours every day - including Fridays - to insure that students understood mathematical concepts.

Imagine a person who could tell a story so well and so hilariously that listeners would laugh until their kleenex, napkins, paper towels and own clothing were soaked from their own tears.

Imagine all of these things in a person, and you start to approach the person of Tom Maguire. Though small in stature, he was bigger than life. Sometimes I think only Shakespeare could have done him justice.

Tom and I began our teaching the same year - 1967: he at the boys' school, Bishop Gibbons, and I at the girls' school, Notre Dame. We knew of each other - he had a much more dramatic presence than I - because of events that involved both schools: faculty meetings, festivals, dances, musicals. In 1975, our schools merged for enrollment reasons, and he and I began our friendship. I think it was in the late 70's that my wife and I saw Shakepeare's *"The Tempest"* at the Mount, the home of Edith Wharton in Lenox, Mass. The play was staged outdoors by Shakespeare and Company. Absolutely stunning was the opening scene when we turned from our lawn-chair seats on the grassy slope to see spotlights flashing on the roof of Edith's home, now rigged to represent Prospero's ship in the storm. The production was outstanding, and two weeks later we returned to the Mount with Tom to see it again. That journey also began the relationship between Deborah and Tom. What followed over the next thirty plus years were wonderful, hilarious, poignant, and exasperating times with Tom as we traveled together to one play or dinner or social gathering after another. During that time, Deborah and Tom became the best of friends, and I often just focused on the driving after a play and listened to the two of them discuss the acting and the staging and the success or failure of the play we had just seen.

Sometime in the mid-80's, Debbie was working as General Counsel for the Division of Substance Abuse Services. One afternoon she received a call from Tom who was in a total panic. "Debbie," in a voice scared and bewildered,

"They won't let me leave. I am at St. Peter's Hospital, and I underwent tests this afternoon. They say that my heart is very bad - five of six arteries are seriously blocked. They won't let me leave." Debbie, who usually had a calming effect on Tom, told him to try to relax, that she would be there as quickly as she could. After calling me in Schenectady, she set out for the hospital and was there in fifteen minutes. A few other close friends whom Tom had called showed up shortly after she did.

In the hospital room, Tom launched into an attack on his own doctor whom he had seen a number of times over the past year because of shortness of breath and some chest discomfort. The doctor, whom we shall call Dr. Q, had diagnosed the problem as a stomach issue and had recommended that Tom take Mylanta regularly as an antidote. When Tom would make reference to him, he was now Dr. Mylanta Q.

The heart surgery didn't take place for over two weeks, and we visited him often. He had been moved from a room right next to the nurses' station to a room that was the farthest away from the station on the floor. The nurses had quickly discovered that he could make quite a racket and was demanding of anyone within earshot. We knew what the nurses were experiencing for we had been many, many times with Tom in public settings - restaurants, lobbies of theaters, subway trains, long bus rides - when his voice and his thoughts became center stage - and the entire room, car, lobby, subway would fixate on this frenetic little, red-faced man who spoke like a machine gun but with much more wit and passion.

Roughly twenty years later on a trip down to see the Yankees with my wife, Tom, and Kristen, a Spanish teacher at the high school, Tom told the story of what had happened to him after he was released from the hospital, a story that almost caused me to cross the thruway divider - I was laughing so hard I couldn't see.

After being driven home from the hospital by a good family friend, Tom settled in back at his home where he lived with his mom and his aunt. Almost immediately, he realized that the prescription he had been given upon his discharge from the hospital was not the medicine that his doctor had prescribed. Instead of calling a relative or friend, he drove himself back to the doctor's office.

Entering the crowded office, he walked right to the check-in desk and said that he had to see the doctor immediately. The woman at the desk told him to take a seat - that there were more than ten people ahead of him. With that he repeated with dramatic emphasis, "I have to see the doctor now," and then ripped his shirt open showing his fresh surgical scar of major demensions. The entire room was in shock. The woman told him to wait right there and scurried to the interior examining rooms. The doctor appeared quickly, took Tom aside, and realized after a few seconds that there was something wrong - a discrepancy that needed to be attended to immediately. The doctor made the adjustment and told Tom to have his driver take him to the pharmacy to get the right prescription. Tom said certainly, left the office, drove himself to the pharmacy, got the right prescription, and then drove himself home. A perfect example of his fierce independence and his refusal to follow proper procedures.

How did Tom's individuality and independent spirit play in the classroom? To what degree did he inspire his students? In looking at one success story, we may catch a glimpse of how Tom affected his students.

Adam loved Mr. Maguire. A bright student, Adam had also starred in school musicals, with Tom as his director. Because he was a top-notch student, I recall Adam many, many days after school with Tom, working on some advanced calculus problems, not immune from an occasional rap on the shoulder from Tom when he felt Adam was being obtuse.

Adam graduated salutatorian and went off to Boston College where he earned his bachelor's and master's in education with a concentration in math. Following his graduation from the master's program, Adam took a position teaching math in a middle school in Boston, and he soon accepted the role of directing the school musicals, one in the fall and one in the spring. He had become the new Mr. Maguire.

One night while chatting with Adam on Facebook, I told him that I was going to work on a profile of Mr. Maguire as part of my memoir. I asked him if he could give me "three keys" to what made Tom a successful teacher. He responded immediately on Facebook - and I was struck by the insights he offered. I will present them verbatim:

"Number 1 - his passion. The man never did anything without passion. He lived and breathed life into each one of the musicals and cared deeply for his students. It was truly a devotion and a calling. Number 2 - his tough love. He knew what your best was and he wouldn't accept anything less, none of this PC bullshit about caring about kids' feelings. If you turned in crap, he told you it was crap, and then told you how capable you were of doing better. I remember the time I got a 70 on a test; instead of saying, you'll do better next time or everyone has a bad day, he wrote, 'YOU are better than this, Adam.' He yelled in rehearsals and pushed you for every ounce you had - and he got it; he pushed for your best and because of his high standards, you knew that what was really under it all was love. Number 3 - his knowledge and his attitude. He beamed with confidence and had a 'If you don't like what I'm doing, screw you' attitude. Maybe I am really saying his confidence. I remember him saying that ND-BG didn't offer AP Calculus exams because he didn't like the test and disagreed with the way they wanted it to be taught. Here's this guy standing up to AP exams. As a teacher now, I look back and thank him for not wasting my time teaching to that stupid test - instead he taught me things that would be useful and made us think. Instead of questioning him, we trusted him. If he thought it was good for us, we also thought it was good for us. Yes, we trusted him - part of that was his confidence. Despite not having children of his own, he was very fatherly. You always knew he was watching over you and would give you the shirt off his back if he could. Unless of course he had a date to see Babs (Barbra Streisand) in concert. His confidence and caring attitude made him trustworthy and a warm presence in the lives of his students."

I thanked Adam for his words, and he added, "Did I nail him - I tried, but honestly no words will ever really do that man justice. I just wear my gold tie on the closing night of our musicals and think of the first man I saw wear the gold bow tie."

Another somewhat different reason Tom lives on in the minds of many of his students is his famous punishment paragraph. When students acted up in his class or just annoyed him, their name would go on the board with a check after it. Each check meant that the student had to write the paragraph ten times; often there were many checks. Here is the legendary paragraph:

"Class is for learning. To accomplish this, I will come to class on time with proper materials, take notes carefully, and be very attentive. To help create an atmosphere conducive to learning, I will refrain from all behavior (such as talking, calling out, turning around) that might prove distracting or disturbing to my classmates or teacher. I will remember that it is my responsibility to learn and the teacher's responsibility to see to it that my behavior does not prevent others from learning. Should this writing assignment prove ineffective in altering my behavior, I understand that additional disciplinary measures will be taken."

Such a well-constructed statement about proper behavior in the classroom - rich sentence variety, parallelism, alliteration, understatement (last sentence) - was written myriads of times, evidenced by the hanging, pained arms of students who exited his room after writing the paragraph over and over and over.

I recall another moment when Tom's talents as a writer flowered. It was his written response to a problematic questionnaire the principal (A Brother who had not worked at all well with the faculty, resulting in a very difficult year) had given us as we anticipated our plans for the following year. The mailbox document had been labeled "Intent Form for all Faculty/Staff." The last check-off item on the intent form read:

Teachers/Counselors. Please check one.

_____ If asked to do/teach something other than what I am presently doing, I am afraid that I could not return here.

_____ If you need me to do something else, I gladly will oblige.

_____ If you need me to do something else, it would be a sacrifice to me, but I would do it.

To which Tom responded:

"I find it impossible to select a choice in this last category. Maybe it's just the wording of the statements that makes this the case. Perhaps I am confused as to the meaning and implications of these choices, but I honestly feel they are offensive. I hope my previous work in this school gives testimony to my willingness to work hard and do my best in both academic and extra-curricular areas. I see no reason why this should not continue to be the case. However, I hestitate to check either the second or third choice for fear that I might end up working on a chain gang to repair the driveway (certainly an area in great need of improvement) or teaching advanced Russian because some "enlightened" administrator feels that offering such a course would attract more students. The first choice does not appeal to me because it seems to be a not so thinly veiled threat that to be unwilling to do "whatever" is asked of me is to choose unemployment at ND-BG. I thought slavery had been

151

abolished by the Thirteenth Amendment. I am finding it difficult to determine the difference between this and the practice employed by sweatshops (a work ethic that seems to be very out of favor with the Catholic Church at least with regard to employers in workplaces other than her own). Before any of this goes much further, it might be helpful to have a discussion or investigation of teachers' rights. Surely the Diocese must have some guidelines in this area.

Finally, at a time when the state is demanding higher standards, it is very important to examine faculty expectations in this light. Can teachers help students meet higher standards if the teachers are overworked or working in areas outside their expertise? Even after all these years it is still not uncommon for me to spend five or six hours a night in teacher-related activities. Surely a larger student load and/ or an increase in number of classes or number of preparations will only increase the burden. Quality instruction requires extensive preparation and high energy. It cannot be maintained when excessive demands are placed upon the teacher. It seems to me that we are rapidly approaching the point of diminishing returns."

Tom had asked me to drop his response off in the principal's mailbox and, on the way to the office, I read it. I was amazed by the humor of his hyperbole and the sharpness of the logic in his blistering response. I liked the way he built his case and then resorted to extreme examples that exposed the choices of the "intent form." His reponse also revealed a person passionately committed to teaching, made a great case for how teachers should be treated, and strongly suggested what makes excellent teachers. Before I turned it into the principal's mailbox, I made a copy for myself.

Memorial Reflections about Tom

After his unexpected and sudden death, the memories of Tom poured in from those who knew him - students, past and present, colleagues, and friends - on a web-site set up by ND-BG. The reflections showed what a great impact he had as a teacher and as a person. What follows are a few memories that reveal his wit and cleverness, one of the reasons he was loved.

Liz Allers recalls one of her favorite moments that showed Tom's wit and character. "Our class was in charge of the food drive. There was one particular day when six people were missing from Calculus in order to count and sort the collected food. When one boy returned briefly to the classroom to get scissors, Mr. Maguire glared at him and asked him why he was skipping Calculus. 'I'm helping the poor!' he exclaimed. 'That's more important than Calculus!' Mr. Maguire retorted, 'If the poor had learned Calculus, they wouldn't be poor.'"

Dana Luvera remembers Mr. Maguire as not only

"an awesome Math teacher, but an inspiring person all around. He was exceptionally funny, sweet, witty, incredibly smart, and passionate. I always loved how he put a sign on the clock in the classroom blocking the time. The sign said, 'Time passes, will you??'"

"I'll never forget my senior year," Joe Putrock says, "when he handed me my Calculus Regents exam. He looked me straight in the eye and said, 'Putrock, the only way you're going to pass this exam is if you eat it.'"

Marlene Goudreau thought of Mr. Maguire's class as a place of fun. "His class was a perfect balance of stand-up, improv, and remarkably solid instruction... I still laugh thinking about some of his classroom antics.... One of my favorite moments came when he was shushing the class so that a certain male student could be heard when answering a question: 'Be quiet, be quiet ... he might say something foolish and I might miss it.'"

McKenzie Weatherwax remembers, "One thing that he told me is something that will always stick in my brain and changed my outlook on math forever. 'I love mathematics. There's always going to be an answer; look past the numbers and letters, and it's simple, black and white. No gray spots.' And the other thing was, 'Shut up, Weatherwax, it's the answer because I said it is the answer.'"

And then the more serious memories, filled with gratitude:

Bob Lindyberg: "In class and life, he was completely unafraid to live by his own terms. When challenged in class by smartass kids (like me), I can't recall that he ever gave an inch, but neither did he let class stop being fun, nor did he discourage having fun. He was equally capable of taming the unruly as he was working one-on-one with anyone who needed help. His diminutive frame contained a giant: a master teacher with a sharp intellect and a huge heart."

Jonathan Sozek: "The classroom was Mr. Maguire's stage, and like all great men of the stage his performance directed your attention to things greater than he himself, inviting you to share the life and love and truth that so obviously motivated all his many pursuits."

Mary Murphy Meachem: "All anyone ever wanted was to be noticed by you, singled out, picked on or embarrassed by you, because if we were we knew that you liked us ... thanks for noticing me!"

Jonathan Signore: "He got me so excited about math that on days that we had tests I would run to his classroom after school to have him tell me his grade. One of the best memories that I have is when another student was in the room practicing problems on the board. Mr. Maguire had finished grading my exam and immediately asked the student in the room to ask me what my average was in class. I responded shyly, '100...' at which Mr. Maguire shouted to the student: 'YOU SEE!! IT IS POSSIBLE!!'"

Kevin Flatt: "In the musicals, he made the ensemble work together, and he could find the right role for every individual; each night we walked off the stage feeling like we were Broadway actors. Mr. Maguire gave us confidence, but he also never let it go to our heads. It was an uncanny ability that he had which would allow our hearts to soar while simultaneously keeping our feet planted firmly on the ground."

Friend and colleague Melanie Anchukaitis concluded her reflection in this way: "A man who loved beauty and found it everywhere: in the flowers on the table, in the voices of his performing students, in the phrasing of a song by Linda Eder, in the praying of a Hail Mary with a group of students, in the triumphant face of a student who has correctly worked through a Math problem. To use a word in Spanish that Tom never did learn, he is the alma of our community at ND-BG. Vivirás en los corazones para siempre. Con mucho cariño, M."

Katie Powers Rose as she gazed at the casket: "I say a Hail Mary because that is what I was taught to do, and silently I recite a prayer of thanks to my still professor. Thanks for the surety, thanks for the proof, thanks for the knowledge of the exact, thanks for the given. I loved the givens. You never knew what you were going to get, but you always knew they were meaningful and solid. Thanks for the boundaries, the order, the proof - proof of value, my value, in a numbered theorem."

A student who signed in as #23, Class of 2002: "I will never forget my first impression seeing this tiny man come up to me after my lazy effort in class and say, 'Young man, I do not care if you can dunk a basketball and you think you will go far with that thing. I am here to tell you that you will not succeed unless you learn to think on a higher level than that rim.' Up until that point no teacher had ever made sense to me on a subject that I never thought I would do well at. And I knew that all the swagger I thought I had, meant nothing to him. I had to show and prove in 'His' class. ... I hope he sees and remembers that lost kid from NYC that he gave a chance to. Thanks, Mr. Maguire, for letting me know then what I know now as a man and in my career, that you have to think on a higher level than that rim."

In her reflection, friend and colleague Joan Horgan prayed that "his fierce love and laughter, that passion and devotion, that unending pursuit of excellence, endure in our hearts and spirits... Oh, what a life we have had the great blessing to share."

And I will close these reflections with Tom's good friend and colleague Linda Niedl: " No doubt Tom created some mathematicians, engineers, accountants, teachers out of the thousands who were privileged to be his students. He created some dancers and singers from the hundreds he directed on stage. But for all, he created a world where others could learn to create, where others could learn to succeed, where others could learn to think, to predict, to be confident, to inspire.

Bravo Bravo Bravo, our dear, dear friend. And blessings on you for eternity, as you find your heaven made of the world you created among us and for us, as you Go in to Your Dance. Live, Tom Maguire, in our hearts and feet and voices, forever."

My final word. People come in and out of our lives constantly; a few remain. Tom was one of the few. In a way he was bigger than life. Shakesperean - more the comic hero but with a strong dose of the seriousness of the tragic hero. He was deadly serious about the beauty and power and incredible value that mathematics brought to this world, and he used his amazing showmanship and brilliant mind to bring students close to his appreciation. Tom and I started teaching the same year: 1967, he with the boys; I with the girls. With his undying energy, I was sure that he would outlive me as a teacher. But that was not to be. And when he died, I wondered what would happen with all that energy he brought every day to the classroom. And then it struck me - his spirit was in each of us, who knew him well. And he would, as Linda said, live on.

Two Shining Moments

Each spring after March Madness - the college basketball tournament, I would play "One Shining Moment," Luther Vandross's song that is a salute to the tournament and especially the winning team. In the study of Homer's *Iliad*, I would present the students with the Greek word aristeia, which means excellence or prowess, especially "the excellence or prowess of an Homeric warrior when he is on a victorious rampage, irresistibly sweeping all before him, killing whomever of the enemy he can catch or whoever stands against him" (Schein 80). After looking at the text for examples of aristeia, I would assign the students a writing of their own ariesteia. I ask them to think of "one shining moment" when everything came together for them, when they were in the flow and just couldn't be stopped. Here are two shining moments from that assignment. The first is entitled "Books" by Brendan O'Connor:

Books

I love books. I love the way they smell, how they feel in your hand, the look of black letters on a clean white page. More than that, I love the ideas in books. My room accumulates piles of books. I borrow books and don't return them because I am gripped with the desire to possess them (or else I forget). And so, you, the reader, can imagine how I must have felt last summer, standing on the steps of a library at Harvard, surrounded by red brick and ivy, listening with rapt attention to the story of a botched attempt to steal the *Gutenberg Bible* (!) that waited just inside, in a glass case next to the *First Folio of Shakespeare* (!).

I thought of little else during the rest of the tour. God had obviously called me to Boston to meet with the two greatest (printed) books in history. Delirious with joy, I relieved John Harvard of some more of his bronze nose and set off across a menacing patch of grass with my mother beside me. Nothing could keep me from my tryst with destiny.

As I crossed the library's threshold, I was met with persecution. "Are you a tourist?" the crusty sentinel asked me. "We don't allow tourists in here."

Tourist? I thought. I have a divine mandate. This man dares call me a tourist?

I channeled my religious zeal into a crafty response. "No, sir. I'm thinking of applying to Harvard in the fall. I'm just here to ... examine your educational facilities."

"Well, you can't get in without a student I.D.," he said. What could I do? I did not have the talisman that he requested. Still, I was not to be vanquished so easily. The objects of my quest were tantalizingly close, only a few rooms away. I knew that to gain entrance I would have to "shuffle off my mortal coil" and rise above the plane of earthly existence. I felt the firey spirit arise within me.

"In that case, is there someone else I could talk to?" I asked the guardian.

"You can see the head librarian, if you like," he told me, gesturing to my right. I marched down the dark hall, filled with purpose, ready to sweep the field and take no prisoners. It turned out that the head librarian was out to lunch. Her replacement was a delicate waif who withered when faced with my piercing gaze. "I don't know ... you see, there's a new policy..."

"I'll just be a moment. I want to look around the Widener Room."

"I don't really have the authority ..."

"There's no problem," I told her. "I'm a prospective student. I won't be long."

"I guess there's no problem ..."

"Thank you." I returned to the entrance where the

sentinel, apparently satisfied, nodded his assent. Advancing up a flight of stairs into the hallowed sanctuary, my eyes were met with a round, warm room lined with rare tomes, and off to one side, a glass case. Having overcome adversity, I looked upon my treasure with my own eyes: the medieval elegance of the first book ever printed and the first edition of the greatest writer who ever lived. The pride of the battle surged in my heart. I had won the day.

The second aristeia is by Rosemary McMahon.

The Night I Danced Alone

I was about ten years old, or around that, I guess. My sisters and I, along with my best friend Elaine and a few other girls, belonged to a sort of dance class at the time. The class was taught by an elderly member of my parish who also belonged to the local chapter of the A.O.H. We learned mostly ceili dances (like square dances), and we also learned the nine steps of the jig, which are the basic moves that make up Irish step dancing. We weren't very good. We didn't kick high, we didn't hold hands right, we laughed and giggled and hung our heads when we performed. But we had fun. Sometimes, though, I would go to the Irish music festivals and see other dancers who did everything perfectly and held their backs straight and their heads high, and I would be jealous. It wasn't the girls with matching headband and fancy dresses I envied; it was the older dancers who performed alone or just in pairs, who didn't have costumes, but had something else, something special and different. The fancy girls' dances seemed mechanical, too practiced, and their dresses too flashy and fluorescent. They seemed snobby and mean, and I felt silly in my homemade skirt and china doll shoes. But the older dancers were very dignified and mature. They were real Irish dancers.

That's what I want to be, I thought, when I grow up.

Those dreams, for the most part, had to be forgotten because I never got to dance alone; I was always with my giggly friends and someone always messed up. I'd come back from a festival with a fresh determination to be serious and mature, but eventually I'd end up dissolving into giddy laughter or making a face at my partner, who was squeezing my hand too hard on purpose.

My family and the others dancers' families used to go to ceilis (social dances) at the senior citizen center in Cobleskill, which I always found fun because I got to run around and play with my friends, and there was even a big long tabletop shuffleboard. One night, for no reason I can recall, I was there alone; that is, I was the only kid there. I was already to be bored out of my skull until I realized that this could be my chance to be like those other dancers, the ones I loved so much. I was by myself, no one was there to make me laugh or mess up.

I was elated, until I began to think that maybe my teacher wouldn't ask me to dance without the other girls being there. Soon I started to almost forget about it; the ceili would be over in just twenty minutes! Finally, my teacher asked me to demonstrate the jig steps. The jig steps! I had never once gotten through all nine without messing up. But I had to do it now; all the old people were waiting, and I knew I'd never get another chance like this.

The music came on, after the traditional five minutes of fumbling with the tapes, and I stood there, waiting. I locked my eyes on a point on the wall, near the ceiling, and told myself firmly not to look down. As the music started, I began to count the familiar beat of the jog - 5, 6, 7, 8, and Go! Step kick, hop back-two-three-four... The first three steps are pretty easy. Then I got to the fourth (Only one rising step, Rose, remember!) I got through it. The fifth step, always a crowd pleaser - hop up, hop back and open, close, kick back, hop back two-three-four. I was kicking as high as I could, trying to remember to keep my arms at my sides. Sixth step (one rising from here on in!) The seventh is a little tricky, kind of off beat - step toe, step toe, heel heel toe stamp kick .... Then all of a sudden I realized, I'm doing it. I heard all the little ooh's and aah's from my delighted elderly spectators. My heart began to soar, and I pressed on - nothing could stop me now! Eighth step, should I quit? We had just learned the ninth step, and we had never done it in performances. But, why not? I had nothing to lose! Step crossover, step crossover, four times in a row, and I didn't lose count. It was over. I had done it. Unable to hold back a huge grin, I took my well-deserved bow, finally releasing my gaze from the point I had fixed on throughout my entire, unprecedented, flawless performance.

Since that night, I've learned many new and complicated dances, I have real dancing shoes (soft and hard) and a fancy velvet costume. I've performed on stage in Proctor's Theater alongside the greatest Irish band on earth. And yet, I have never felt so proud as I did standing in that little room on a side street in Cobleskill, listening to the thunderous applause of my tiny audience and feeling for all the world like a real Irish dancer.

Words That Mattered:

I have chosen eleven quotations from literature I have taught that spoke eloquently to me. In these words truth rings.

1. "We shall not cease from exploration, and the end of all our exploring will be to arrive where we started and know the place for the first time" (Eliot 145).

In a poetry course in college, I was introduced to T. S. Eliot. After studying the well-known Eliot poems, "Prufrock," "Hollow Men," "Ash Wednesday," etc., our professor made reference to a longer work called "Four Quartets." I remember reading through the poem and being both dazzled by the language and baffled by the thought. Certain lines were magnetic for me, lines that were like pebbles dropped in a pond - they rippled out and each time I returned to the lines, the ripple extended further. When I think of the line I cited from the section called "Little Gidding" in Four Quartets, I reflect on the fact that every step we take is both a step onward and outward in our journey and a step inward and backward - in retrospectively seeing the past more clearly.

The Eliot quotation takes on personal significance in my life at one moment in particular. From my earliest memory, our family said the rosary together. The moral force behind that ritual was my mother, who was our guide in spiritual matters. Regardless of what was going on in our lives, my mother always called us to kneel together and say the rosary. On long car trips we could not kneel, but we still said the rosary. My mother lived a fairly long life - 86 years old - until she had a serious heart attack. At Memorial Hospital, the family arrived in different time frames. Both of my brothers were in difficult situations that required time. And so my mother was kept alive by a machine until all were there. We stood around the bed, children and spouses, and held hands. Then together we said the "Hail Mary." As we said the prayer, I thought of how strong a presence my mother had been in our lives, I thought of her always encouraging us to do the right thing, and I thought of the prayer that was the most important to her, one that she had taught to us, the "Hail Mary." The closing of the prayer is "Holy Mary, Mother of God, pray for us sinners, now and at the hour of our death. Amen." Mary had been her intercessor her entire life, and now we were asking Mary to intercede in prayer for our mother. This moment and this prayer brought an entire life to its fulfillment. I had arrived at my start and now understood more clearly.

2. "But this too is true: stories can save us" (O'Brien 255).

These words are spoken by the narrator of Tim O'Brien's *The Things They Carried*. From Odysseus to Huck Finn to Holden Caulfield to Tim O'Brien, we see over and over the ringing truth that stories have the power to save us. Odysseus, forever the tale spinner, as he wends his long, circuitous journey home; Huck, traveling down the beautiful and dangerous Mississippi into the dark South, reinventing himself along the way; Holden, who would call himself a phony for doing it, fabricating tales about his feats and his failures; and Tim O'Brien, seeing the nightmare of war, retelling the stories of soldiers he knew and giving them life, and dreaming alive one young girl by the name of Linda who died of brain cancer. "She was dead. I understood that. After all, I'd seen her body, and yet as a nine-year-old I had begun to practice the magic of stories" (272). And when he thinks more about Linda, he imagines himself skating with her, "moving fast, riding the melt beneath the blades, doing loops and spins, and when I take a high leap into the dark and come down thirty years later, I realize it is as Tim trying to save Tim's life with a story" (273). When I think of my years teaching, I can recall no greater bonding agent and unifier of people and memories than the stories told in class by me and by the students who were present, stories that nutured and that revealed character and that brought us together.

3. "It is always a matter, my darling,/ Of life or death, as I had forgotten. I wish/ What I wished you before, but harder" (Wilbur 5).

The last stanza of Richard Wilbur's poem "The Writer" touches the core of life. The poem is about the speaker's daughter trying to write a story, with the speaker listening to the stopping and starting of her typewriter in "her room at the prow of the house." He has been climbing the stairs to her room and has paused. As he listens, he wishes "her a lucky passage." Typewriter keys are heard and then silence. In the silence he recalls a "dazed starling" that was trapped in his daughter's room two years earlier, and how he and his daughter slipped into the room and lifted the window sash. Then they retreated and watched through the crack of the door as the starling attempted to escape through the window. And though many attempts were failures, leaving the bird "humped and bloody," the bird finally flew a "smooth course for the right window" and cleared "the sill of the world." That is when he utters the final lines. How true they are!! The road to clearing the sill and telling your story is not an easy one - one must try and try and try. And if one does not clear the sill, if one cannot tell her story, then the voice is lost. Yes, it is "always a matter of life or death." If you can't tell your story, you remain trapped in the room and lost.

4. "Still, I would not/ die without delivering a stroke,/ or die ingloriously, but in some action/ memorable to men in days to come" (Homer *Iliad* 525).

No purer moment is there to represent the Greek concept of fame (kleos) than this one with Hector as he faces Achilles in the climax of the *Iliad*. He knows in his heart and soul that he cannot defeat Achilles, the greatest fighter on the battlefield. He is alone, the last hope for the city of Troy, in a final battle that he should never have had to fight, except for the moral failure of his brother Paris in stealing Helen away from Menelaus. All he can do now is to make his end noble and give his all against the man who is filled with wrath over Hector's slaying in battle Achilles' closest friend Patroclus. Hector knows also that Achilles will have no mercy and will not respect his fallen remains.

Fighting Achilles is a moment that makes the doomed Hector live forever in our minds. Rarely in my life have I had a task or witnessed a moment that seemed daunting or overwhelming without Hector and this moment with Achilles flashing into my mind. How does one go forward!

The day before my father died, I had called my sister, a nurse, to ask if she needed any help with my dad. She was staying at our family home with my dad and mom. She said, "No, I will be fine." As I was talking, my wife was nodding yes to my question of should we go out to help.

And so we did. Thank God.

My father, who was still a big man, slid off his chair onto the floor three times during the night. Only the three of us together could lift him back up to a comfortable position. At this moment in his life, there was nothing we could do except try to give him a sense of dignity and comfort. That was all.

5. "She would have been a good woman," the Misfit said, "if it had been somebody there to shoot her every minute of her life" (O'Connor 669).

The character known as the Misfit in Flannery O'Connor's short story "A Good Man is Hard to Find," represents the extreme someone can reach in life. The Misfit, a killer, has escaped from prison and encountered a family of five. The family's grandmother, a self-centered and annoying woman, confronts the Misfit.

She tries to make him think of Jesus and thus shift his thinking and ways.

The Misfit is a hard-nosed pragmatist who insists that if Jesus actually did what he did, raise the dead and perform miracles, then "It's nothing for you to do but throw away everything and follow Him, but if he didn't do all those things then it's nothing for you to do but enjoy the few moments you got left the best you can -- by killing somebody or burning down his house or doing some other meanness to him. No pleasure but meanness" (668). The grandmother becomes passionate about the role of Jesus in the Misfit's life. But the Misfit speaks the pragmatist's ultimate line about Jesus's actions, "If I had been there, I would have known, and I wouldn't be like I am now" (668). At that moment the grandmother reaches out and touches the Misfit who recoils and shoots her three times through the chest.

The reader wonders if meanness and frustration is all that the Misfit can respond with, but his statement has a powerful ring. Though one can argue that the grandmother is merely trying to save her own life with her pleading, one could also see in the Misfit's line that only at certain moments in our lives - when we are confronted with the reality of dying - do we take our lives seriously. We feel a shotgun on our neck, and the whole world shifts.

6. "See better, Lear," (Act 1, sc. 1, 180).

In Act I of the play, King Lear banishes from his kingdom the one true daughter, Cordelia, because she does not attempt to enter the ring with her sisters and proclaim how much she loves her father, thus earning portions of his kingdom. Cordelia, when asked to express her love, says simply the word, "Nothing." When Lear in disbelief says, "Nothing will come from nothing, speak again," Cordelia says, "I love your Majesty/Acccording to my bond, no more nor less." Cordelia can say nothing to match the false expressions of hyperbolic love that her sisters have uttered.

And so she chooses not to bargain with her father over gifts that depend upon how much each daughter can express her love. At this moment, with his life in jeopardy, Lear's faithful supporter Kent steps forward to make the case for Cordelia. Lear, teetering on the edge, says to Kent, "Peace, Kent, / Come not between the dragon and his wrath." When Kent tries again by saying, "Thy youngest daughter does not love thee least,..." Lear responds, "Out of my sight." It is at this point that Kent says, "See better, Lear, and let me still remain / The true blank of thine eye." Let me remain at the center of your vision (Act I, sc. 1, lines 135-181).

No two words capture the theme of *King Lear* better than the admonition to Lear to "see better." In his need to hear how much each daughter loves him, Lear has used love as a bargaining chip. He cannot see that two daughters are masters at this game. By the end of the play, Lear will "see better" who was true and know the cost of blindness. As a teacher I have had a number of occasions in which I should have seen better. Because my attention was on my own needs and agenda, I missed what was happening in front of me. Sometimes a Kent appeared, often my wife Deborah, and her words I did not always heed. In time, sometimes too late, I saw.

7. "They're a rotten crowd," I shouted across the lawn. "You're worth the whole damn bunch put together" (Fitzgerald 154).

I always wanted to stand up and cheer for Nick Carraway as he said this line to Gatsby. Holden Caulfield's favorite word is "phony," usually ascribed to those who are putting on airs and pretending to be something they are not. If one were to measure Gatsby by Holden's standards, Gatsby would be a major "phony." Gatsby's childhood, his education, his source of money, and his lavish parties all slowly unravel to reveal Gatsby as a very different person - "I am not what I am." And yet what draws us closer and closer to Gatsby is our growing awareness that there is a method and a purpose in his madness. All he has done and all he is doing is motivated by one thing - his love for Daisy Buchanan. From the moment he met her as a young debutante in Louisville, Gatsby, a soldier in the army, was smitten, and because she was from a wealthy family, he began to reinvent a character he felt would be worthy of her and her world. As he departs for the war, they vow to be reunited when he returns. She does not wait and marries the wealthy Tom Buchanan.

It is Gatsby's love for her and his desire to recapture her that motivates everything that he does. His goal is to win her back by making her realize that he is the one she wants. That Daisy is not equal to the person he imagined and betrays Gatsby in the end makes Gatsby a haunting and tragic character.

What Nick saw in Gatsby "was an extraordinary gift for hope, a romantic readiness such as I have never found in any other person...." In his hope and in his relentless pursuit of love, Gatsby rose above "the whole damn bunch" (Fitzgerald 2).

8. "Where is God now?"

'And I heard a voice within me answer him':

"Where is He? Here He is - He is hanging here on this gallows..." (Wiesel 62).

For over ten years, my wife and I have driven to Weston, Vermont, for the Good Friday service that is at the center of Holy Week. A socially conscious order with a strong link to Third World countries, the Weston Monks celebrate the holy day with a great deal of music and readings of social awareness and situations of suffering around the globe. I had taught Elie Wiesel's book *Night*, the account of his experience in World War II and the horror of the concentration camps. The book explores Wiesel's great struggle with God and the presence of God in such overwhelming darkness. On one particular day the SS had hanged three people who had not revealed information that they deemed necessary. One of the three had been a young boy. With the noose around the necks of the two adults and the boy, someone behind the narrator (Eliezer, who in many ways is Wiesel) asked, "Where is God? Where is He?" The chairs are tipped and the nooses grab hold of each neck. Within a short time, the adults are dead, but the small child lives for more than a half hour, dying in slow agony. That is the moment the question is asked, "Where is God now?" The response at that moment in the Church at Weston was stunning - maybe the spoken word has more power, maybe at that moment I was ready to hear the words. The voice of the narrator says, "Where is He? Where is He? Here He is - He is hanging here on the gallows..." What makes this response so intense and so strong is that the answer speaks of both darkness and of hope. One could say God is not present because the young boy has suffered beyond belief and there was no one to save him - the darkest hour; one could also say that the young boy is a perfect representative of God, who suffered and died for us on the Cross. If you look closely, you will see Jesus.

9. "One day you finally knew/ what you had to do, and began, / though the voices around you kept shouting their bad advice" (Oliver 114).

Whether it be Huck, Biff Loman, Elizabeth Bennett, or Nora Helmer, there comes that moment when it is time to make the decision that will allow one to enter his or her own world. Mary Oliver's "The Journey" is a poem that I have shared with friends, especially those going through difficult times. It is a poem of personal liberation, how difficult it is to free oneself from the "voices shouting bad advice" and "the old tug on the ankles." Each outside voice crying, "Mend my life!" And the determination to go on against the melancholy and "the wind prying with its stiff fingers." The pressures that family, friends, and the culture in general apply are so strong that one marvels how anyone can find his own freedom. The poem speaks of the time "already late enough and a wild night," with "the road full of fallen branches and stones." Can one overcome the obstacles and see one's way in the darkness? But if you persevere, the voices start to weaken and then "the stars began to burn / through the sheets of clouds." Finally one can begin to see and then "There was a new voice/ which you slowly/ recognized as your own," and that voice was yours and it would be your "company" as "you strode deeper and deeper/ into the world,/ determined to do / the only thing you could do - determined to save/ the only life that you could save." The poem speaks of those raw existential moments when people really choose their authentic selves. In the end, no one can make this choice for you. It is your journey in your dark night of the soul, and your choice that will result in the light that will show you your way. Huck, Biff, Elizabeth, and Nora all made that journey.

10. "Whoever you are, I have always depended on the kindness of strangers" (Williams 142).

One of the most memorable lines in contemporary literature, Blanche Dubois's words to the Doctor who has come to take her to a mental instution reveal so much about her state of mind. Blanche, now totally immersed in her fantasy world after suffering the brutal attack by Stanley, believes that her gentleman friend Shep Huntleigh is coming to take her to the land of castles and oil wells. But it is not Shep Huntleigh who arrives; it is the mental institution's doctor. Blanche at first retreats in horror and has to be subdued by the Doctor's assistant. But when the doctor looks down at Blanche with gentleness and caring eyes, she responds with her words. For the moment she has become what she wanted all to think she was - a lady of dignity and grace. What makes the line reverberate so strongly is what it says about Blanche and her future. The play has come to expose her in Mitch's words as a liar - "Lies, lies, inside and out, all lies." Blanche makes the argument to Mitch that she "didn't lie in her heart." But too late for Blanche - Mitch sees her now as only a cheap trick. Stanley in the next scene will put the final nail in the coffin by raping Blanche.

The power of the line, "I have always depended on the kindness of strangers" speaks to a fear that Blanche had when she opened her heart to Mitch in an earlier scene and told him about an ugly event from her past. When she discovered that her husband Allen was gay, she cruelly attacked him on the dance floor by telling him that he disgusted her. As a result, Allen stuck a revolver in his mouth and killed himself. Blanche accepts the blame for the awful deed. In telling Mitch of her awful failure with another human being, she hopes that he will not do to her what she did to Allen, if he finds out about her past. Her hope is punctured when Mitch does find out about Blanche's past. Thus the "kindness of strangers" is in a way all that Blanche has; for she knows that if a person she cares about finds out about her, she will be rejected. All she has now are strangers.

11. "I know who I am, kid" (Miller 138).

The road has been so long for Biff Loman to this momentous utterance in his journey. His father, Willy Loman, is dead, and he and his family, along with Charlie, his neighbor, and Bernard, Charlie's son, have gathered at the gravesite. Charlie, Happy, and Linda offer their reflections on what Willy Loman's life has meant. Charlie sees Willie's life as his inability to be a salesman anymore - when people stop "smiling back - that's an earthquake." Happy, Willy's other son, believes that Willy had a "good dream" - "to come out number one man." And Happy will continue to fight to prove Willy right. Linda remains baffled over Willy's life and death. "Why did you do it?" she asks. "I search and I search and I search, and I can't understand it." Biff has weathered many storms in his life. He has drifted, been in jail, tried to find himself in different jobs, and has always come home with his spirit unsettled. His tension with his father, once his hero, is always foregrounded in the play - as Willy keeps pressing Biff, whether in the present with a potential sales job or in the past with his skills as an athlete, to shoot for the sky. And then the play opens up the conflict in a climatic flashback as Biff, a high school student who has failed his Regents math, comes to Boston seeking Willy's help. His opening statement, "Dad, I let you down" proves bitterly ironic when Biff discovers his hero, his Dad, with a hooker. Biff's life is never the same again. By the end of the play, after his confrontation with his father about filling him with dreams to be number one man, he finally screams at this father, "Pop, I'm nothing. I'm nothing," and collapses in utter exhaustion.

King Lear had told Cordelia that nothing shall come from nothing. Biff's nothing is an everything that marks the beginning of his life, freed from the shackles of Willy's dreams, free to build a new life. "I know who I am."

The Dinner to Honor Me

On November 28, 2014, Notre Dame-Bishop Gibbons honored me with a dinner, which featured four speakers who have played key roles in my life: Dr. Brian Hickey, former student and now exercise science professor at Florida A & M; Antonio Delgado, former student, Rhodes Scholar, Harvard Law grad and now practicing attorney in New York City; Brother Kevin Griffith, Province Leader of the Edmund Rice Christian Brothers and close friend; and Linda Neidl, long-time colleague in the English department. In addition, James Tedisco, Member of the New York State Assembly, a graduate of Bishop Gibbons and a former teaching colleague at ND-BG, presented me with a Citation from the New York State Assembly. The opening prayer was delivered by my brother, Father Leo O'Brien, and the concluding comments for the evening were given by Bishop Howard Hubbard. I found the evening to be very moving and the speeches to be most thoughtful and personal.

My speech was really divided into two parts: the first part was one of personal experiences and memories from the early years, spiced with tales of humor and stories of teaching challenges. The second was a long, kind of free-verse narrative of my career as a teacher, highlighting special moments and special people. What follows is the second part of my speech:

"The Essence of 47"

And so Room 6 was empty
with this exception
On my desk
I had placed
a piece of driftwood
pulled years ago from the waters
of Raquette Lake.
Against the driftwood now
I had placed three items
To the left - a picture of me
in first grade
in my one-room school house.
Resting at the center of the driftwood
my tattered copy of Homer's *Odyssey*.
To the right -
Tim O'Brien's *The Things They Carried*
"Stories can save our lives," he said.
Standing back I snap a picture
of my display
And then begin to place
the four items in a box.
I feel kind of sad but very happy too

like those nights when you drift off to sleep
after a good and rewarding day.

Notre Dame High School in 1967
A little rocky starting
that first year
but
the school had the feel
of a world I knew and understood -
Home.
When home means so much to you
You see it in new places
and I did.
In the Notre Dame Sisters I taught with
"Would you like to join us for dinner?"
"Do you need a little extra money?"
"Let Father Nabozny take your class tomorrow
He has some guidance work he can do
with the students."
Sister Kavanaugh, Sister Keily
Sister Senesac, Sister Lucey.
Sister Flanagan, Sister Vivian
Bright, forward-thinking women
Complemented so well
by bright teachers like Melanie Anchukaitis
Claudia Eagan, Jeff Laing,

Betty Bogaardus, Connie Sorrentino
- and of course Father Nugent
Friday afternoons in the faculty room -
a drink or two, stories, laughter -
It was good.

And the students who challenged
a teacher to climb
Merton's The Seven Story Mountain
The Education of Henry Adams
And reach out
The Way We Were
"Notre Dame girls - go to wardrobe
The ballroom scene starts in one hour."
Lincoln Center coming to our little stage -
theater, opera, chamber music.
Could flight really take place
on our small stage?
Yes - said Peter Pan.

And 1975 - the merger
of Notre Dame and Bishop Gibbons.
Hospitality and home
still reigned
In Brother Ed Roepke
and his evenings of German cuisine
Dinner with the Brothers -

Pi McDonough, Damien Ryan, Eugenio Delorenzo
Brendan Moffett, Gene Nardi, Tom O'Connor,
James DePiro, Kevin Griffith, and Joe Fragala
"And now join us for prayer."
And the more you feel welcomed and accepted
the more your own world takes on that tone.
Rocking chairs, rugs, photographs, posters,
Irish sweaters -
I mean - how was home different from school?
It really wasn't.
Come on in
We've got a little music for you here.
Dean Martin, Billy Joel, Nat King Cole.
If you wanted to see depression
lift in an instant
The Bee Gee's "Staying Alive"
would be the remedy.
Come on in
We will be doing
a little vocab today
We'll start a book
I think you will love
And do some writing
Exchange some ideas
and laugh a little.
To get the class started

let me tell you about
a Johnny Carson story
from last night.
Johnny, Dick Cavett, SNL
How many classes opened
with a skit from SNL?
"I live in a van down by the river."
And don't forget "Chopping Broccoli"
and the Church Lady
Gilda Radner and the bawdy
and brash Roseanne Roseannadanna.
And whatever Will Farrell did
on Saturday Night.
Yes - humor relaxes the soul.

Sometimes the mood of the class
became very serious and dark
Listening to Willy Loman
trying to find an answer
in his own memories.
"Yes," it was true
what Thoreau said,
"Most men lead lives of quiet desperation."
Serious when they read about Huck's choice
to risk his soul for the slave Jim
for the students had seen

along with Huck
that Jim was human
and a man of dignity
Serious and inspired when they read
of Antigone's audacity
And aware of the dark direction
life can turn
as they watched Blanche Dubois
make her final exit.

And there were moments missed
students whose voices were not heard
Whose eyes I had not looked into.
"Mr. O'Brien, do you remember me?
I was in your class."
The face might come back
but I knew in my heart and soul
that I had missed them
Eclipsed by others perhaps -
a stillness I had not heard
'You should have seen better,"
an echo from Lear.

Other losses too
painful and yet
it was then that you felt
the community coming together-

giving you strength
through their presence and their prayer.
Loved ones gone -
Tommy and Andres and Jordan
and Mark and Ron and Mike - and more
And when things came too close
The strong arms of Katheen Duff
and Monica Murphy and so many faculty
supporting one another at times of loss.
Tom and Irene and Cathy and Brother Joe
And Kendra's Joe
Great loss brings people together
to heal and gain strength for another day
a deeper communion.

Moments of transformation and enlightenment
"Ok, Class, today we are going
to start reading 'Sonny's Blues.'
It's a long story - probably
will take us two days.
It's the story of two brothers
and how one - the so-called succcessful one -
the teacher- comes to see the beauty
of his brother - the one people
saw as a failure ...
Omar, would you start

with the first paragraph -
read a few paragraphs and then
we will move on to another reader."
Omar started
and the class grew quiet
and the feeling in the room shifted.
Omar was reading
as if it was his story
pure and completely at one
with the mind of James Baldwin.
The following day Omar
continued reading
and finished the story.
He had led us all into a new understanding
of what the words and the story meant.

"Tim, I have to talk with you
about Sunday's poetry reading
at the library.
Where are you?
Where?
In a tree in the park reading *Les Mis*?
Where is this park?
Stay right where you are -
I will be right over."
And so I drove to the park

and yes, there was Tim
nestled high up
between two branches of a huge oak
reading *Les Mis*.

Mock Trial team wins again
and again and again
What an amazing accomplishment
for our small school
Linda and Melanie
and their great cast of students.
I always take pride in posting wins
Especially beating Niskayuna
three times - last year.
And winning State Championships
in Girls' Hoop
and Boys' Cross Country.

"The Rhodes Scholars this year
include a Capital District resident -
Antonio Delgado."
What a superb achievement!
And Doc Hickey is back once again
giving the school two, three, four days
however many he can fit in -
Days of inspiration firing the students up
To achieve academically and athletically.

And sports' wins that one cannot explain
1982 - an athlete dies on a November Friday
after a long battle with cancer.
And the Gibbons team - under Coach Blaha
elects to play that evening.
The opponent - Albany High - is much more talented
and physical -
At the end of three quarters
the score reads: Albany 57, Gibbons 39.
Then the whole world shifts -
Albany can't score
And Gibbons can't miss!
At the buzzer a shot is launched
from Mark Nealon - YES!!
Gibbons 59, Albany 57
Gibbons 59, Albany 57!!
Coach Blaha said he had never
seen a game like this before.
And the papers the next day sang out
"Miraculous Win at Gibbons" and "Miracle at Gibbons."

On that same court over 25 years later
Philippe Petit, the man who walked
between the Twin Towers,
showed the Gibbons students -
by using the lines on the basketball court -

how he crossed the cable
between the World Trade Center Towers
taking one section at a time.
An impossible task - and he did it!

"Don't ever give up," Jimmy V said.
"Don't ever give up."
What a great line!
And I loved how he summed up a full day:
"You laugh, you cry, you think -
you do those three things each day - that's a full day."

While attending a funeral of a colleague's Dad
a few weeks ago in Buffalo
I drove past a Catholic High School
a number of times - underneath the name
of the school, there was a bright sign
that read, "Not just a school."

That's the way I have come to think
about Notre Dame-Bishop Gibbons
not just a school, but a place
where people can laugh and cry and think
and feel that they matter
and that their voice is heard.
In so many ways
ND-BG remains my home.

As I close this memoir, one song is playing through my mind, "The End," written by Lennon and McCartney. The line "And in the end, the love you get is equal to the love you give." In the world of teaching, I believe this is the truth. If you approach your students with a sense of openness and fairness and a sense that each and every one matters, then the students see that and respond in kind. Often the response is not immediate - one of the realities of teaching - but in time, what usually emerges is the awareness that he cared for me and wanted me to do well. I also believe that at the heart of the world of teaching is the opportunity it offers each of us to nurture and foster the voice that is in each person. We are very fortunate to have this opportunity. The poem "The Writer" is so conscious of this reality, as the speaker concludes, "It is always a matter, my darling, / Of life or death, as I had forgotten. I wish / What I wished you before, but harder."

Each person needs to tell his or her story, needs a voice, needs an ear, needs a community. Stories are what make up the fabric of our being.

The essential role of stories in our lives is beautifully captured in the film version of J.R.R Tolkien's *The Two Towers*. Sam, Frodo's loyal and wise companion, responds to Frodo who is near despair about fulfilling the Quest to destroy the ring that has demonic power.

Frodo: I can't do this, Sam.

Sam: I know. It's all wrong. By rights we shouldn't even be here. But we are.

It's like in the great stories, Mr. Frodo. The ones that really mattered. Full of darkness and danger, they were. And sometimes you didn't want to know the end. Because how could the end be happy? How could the world go back to the way it was when so much bad had happened? But in the end, it's only a passing thing, this shadow. Even darkness must pass. A new day will come. And when the sun shines it will shine out the clearer.

Those were the stories that stayed with you. That meant something, even if you were too small to understand why. But I think, Mr. Frodo, I do understand. I know now. Folk in those stories had lots of chances of turning back, only they didn't. They kept going. Because they were holding on to something.

Frodo: What are we holding onto, Sam?

Sam: "That's there's some good in this world, Mr. Frodo ... and it's worth fighting for" (The Two Towers 2002 Film).

A Retrospective

Father Paul Roman, diocesan priest and chaplain of Notre Dame-Bishop Gibbons from 1976 to 1980, had a recurring question he would ask a student whose attention he had gained, "My dear brother in Christ, are you going to replace me in my old age?" That question hits at the heart of the idea of the future for the Church and for Catholic Schools. In 1968, the enrollment at Bishop Gibbons High School was over 800 boys; at Notre Dame High School, the enrollment was over 600 girls. I know that a tuition increase of $200 at Bishop Gibbons the following year caused a significant drop in enrollment. In 1975 because of declining enrollments and the growing relationship between the two schools, a merger took place and Notre Dame-Bishop Gibbons was formed with an enrollment, as I remember, of somewhat over 700 students. Today, the enrollment at the school is below 300 students, and people keep searching for ways to increase the student population.

I understand fully that the decline in religious vocations has had a major impact on the Church and the schools. When I started at Notre Dame, there were only a handful of lay faculty on staff; the rest were Notre Dame Sisters. But in the late 60's and early 70's, the Sisters were pulled in different directions, mostly to assist the poor in different capacities, some to return to secular life. Today there is one Notre Dame Sister left in the high school, Sister Jeanne Fielder, who has been there for over 20 years. In 1967, the number of Christian Brothers working at Bishop Gibbons was 14. The last Christian Brother to be on staff at Notre Dame-Bishop Gibbons was Brother Joseph Fragala who left the school in 2008 to go to a House of Brothers in the city of New Orleans and work with the poor and troubled.

Another reality that has caused change and affected long-term commitment has been finance. Five years ago, a young teacher named Dan joined the staff at the high school. He was blessed with many talents. He was a good teacher and related well with the students, he was a musician, he was a professional photographer, and he was committed spiritually. As I saw the end of my career approaching, I viewed him as one who would carry on the mission. And when I did retire, he took over much of the teaching program I had. But then finances and the needs of his family became a priority. With a third child on the way, he was scraping to get by: teaching, working as campus minister, managing the yearbook, running his photography business - he was exhausted. So when an offer came to take another teaching position at a significant jump in salary, he had to take it. And I totally understood and honestly wished him all the best. I have seen Dan's story over and over in my teaching career at ND-BG: Gifted teachers who stayed three to five years and then for financial reasons moved on to other schools.

Sometimes, however, I am puzzled over patterns that have shifted. Over and over again during the last thirty years or so, I have been with graduates of our high school at parties or reunions. They speak glowingly of their years at ND-BG, their love of the teachers, their memories of good times, their successes and their failures. Yet, even though they were for the most part successful in their careers, they have not sent their own children to the school they speak so well of. I ask myself why. A few thoughts: The belief that a Catholic education is vital in this world has faded, and many find that the Church is not relevant in their world. Certainly tuiton is a factor - $7000 a year is a drain for most people. Perhaps the decline in the numbers of the two religious orders teaching in the school was a factor for some - the parents having known and experienced the Brothers and Sisters. Maybe the fact that declining enrollment resulted in weaker athletic teams. I used to think that if all the athletes who were children of Gibbons graduates had come to Gibbons, we would have had the best teams in the entire area. Community and peer pressure? "My children are going to Niskayuna or Burnt Hills, of course. They offer so much more." And that was true and still is. But I have thought many times that if one were to look at just the core curriculum, Notre Dame-Bishop Gibbons was often as strong as any of the public schools. And as one parent told me, whose son had gone to Georgetown, earned his Doctorate at the University of Arizona, and was now teaching at Arizona State, "I don't think he could have accomplished any more in any school than he did at ND-BG. In theater, sports, community service, and academics, the school served him very well."

Why did I stay? On a few occasions, I was asked if I would like to teach in local public schools. On three occasions, I was asked if I wanted to take a position with the State Ed Department. I said no to all. When I earned my doctorate from SUNYA in 1995, my director said to me, "Now you take this degree and go to Brother Principal and ask for the big raise." I looked at him, and we both laughed. Still he wondered why I would not want to look for a position teaching English in college. A few years later, I took a position as an adjunct teaching two courses at the College of St. Rose, which I did for a few years. Still, I never left Notre Dame-Bishop Gibbons, continuing to teach at least three courses at the high school.

So why did I stay for forty seven years in the school? From the beginning, I sensed that within the frame of Catholicism, I had freedom. Once I was established, I felt that I could be trusted to choose texts that challenged the students. From the Notre Dame Sisters, I experienced respect and tremendous support. When the two schools merged, there was a period of adjustment - for one, the Christian Brothers had taught only boys up until this merger. For another, the curriculum and approach to learning differed dramatically between the two schools: Bishop Gibbons was for the most part traditional in its approach to education - nothing experimental or avant garde. Notre Dame had been a center of dramatic experiments, allowing students to choose their own style of learning: individual - one on one; small group in a seminar approach; traditional classroom. Yet, after some turbulent waters, the ship of education began to sail well at the merged school. And I felt comfortable and secure in doing what I loved to do: being in the presence of an eager, excited group of students and bringing some fuel to their fires in the form of books, writing, cinema, and good discussion. And finding a number of new friends among the Brothers and lay faculty in the school.

When you have been in a school for some time and when your reputation is favorable, your life takes on a kind of inner ease and peace. You begin to build a reputation and because of that you have a head start on each new group of students you encounter each year. When you walk through the halls, it is as if you know the whole world, and that in itself speaks volumes about school size. On one occasion a number of years ago, one of our grads who was attending

Schenectady Community College popped in after school. He had brought a friend he had met at the SCCC. We chatted and the friend mentioned that he had graduated from a local suburban school. I asked him what the size of his graduating class was - he said, "I think it was about 800." I asked him how many students in his graduating class he knew. He said, "About 100." Then he added, "There were people who walked across the stage that I had never seen before." The Gibbons grad's class numbered 47. He knew each and every graduate.

When I was getting ready to go to high school, a new school opened about four miles from my home. Many of my childhood friends were going there, and they were very excited. I said to my mother, "Mom, can I go to Tamarac High School?"

She looked at me and said, "You are going to Catholic Central High School." I really knew the answer before I asked the question. In fact, as soon as Our Lady of Victory School in Troy had opened, my brother and I left the one-room school house we had studied in for four years and went there. Those choices happened because my mother believed deeply that the Faith mattered and that if given the opportunity to sit in an educational environment which had the teachings of Jesus Christ as its fundamental foundation, nothing could be better. I am happy that she was the catalyst in my life for Catholic education. Obviously more than I ever could have anticipated - forty seven years teaching in a Catholic High School.

The Mission Statement of Notre Dame-Bishop Gibbons begins with this line: "Notre Dame-Bishop Gibbons Catholic School is a faith-filled community dedicated to the belief that learning is a life-long process and that Christian commitment never ceases." The Mission Statement ends with these words: "Inspired by the wisdom of the Gospel and aware of Catholic traditions, our graduates can respond to the challenges of the future with knowledge, compassion, and conviction." Many of those who have dedicated and committed themselves to Notre Dame-Bishop Gibbons believe in the truth of these words. In a world often in disarray and dissension, those words and their meaning provide a vision and a frame that offers hope and light. As the aspiration from Blessed Edmund Rice goes, "Live Jesus in our hearts forever."

Works Cited

Ashe, Arthur. Days of Grace. New York: Alfred A. Knopf. 1993.

Baldwin, James. "Sonny's Blues." The Story and Its Writer. Ed. Ann Charters.Boston: Bedford/St. Martin. 2003. 25-47. Print.

Bingham, Howard, and Max Wallace. Muhammad Ali's Greatest Fight. New York: M. Evans and Company, Inc. 2000.

Cavett, Dick. Talk Show. New York: Times Books, 2010.

Crapsey, Adelaide. "On Seeing Weather-beaten Trees." Modern American Poetry. Bartleby.com. Wed 22 October 2015.

Drumm, Russell. "Aloha, My Fearless Friend." East Hampton Star. 21 Jan 2010 B 1, B4.

"Ebony and Ivory." SNL. 22 Feb. 2007. Television.

Eliot, T.S. The Complete Poems and Plays. New York: Harcourt, Brace, and World, 1962.

Fitzgerald, F. Scott. The Great Gatsby. New York: Collier Books, 1980.

"Ghetto Gospel." From Tupac Shakur's Loyal to the Game. 2004. CD.

Homer. The Iliad. Trans. Robert Fitzgerald. Garden City: Anchor, 1962.

- -. The Odyssey. Trans. Robert Fitzgerald. Garden City: Anchor, 1974.

Johnson, Mark, prod. Playing for Change. Notes on "Stand by Me." StarCon, LLC d/b/a Hear Music, 2009. CD.

Kennedy, Robert. "On the Assassination of Martin Luther King." Indianapolis, Indiana. 4 April 1968. John F. Kennedy Presidential Library and Museum. Speech.

- -. "Tribute to John F. Kennedy at the Democratic National Convention." Atlantic City, New Jersey. 27 Aug. 1964. John F. Kennnedy Presidential Library and Museum. Speech.

Kennedy, Ted. "Eulogy for his Brother Robert." St. Patrick's Cathedral, New York 5 June 1968. John F. Kennedy Presidential Library and Museum. Speech.

King, Martin Luther. "I've Been to the Mountaintop." Memphis, Tennessee. 3 April 1968. "American Rhetoric." Speech.

Lennon, John and Paul McCartney. "The End." Metrolyrics.

Miller, Arthur. <u>Death of a Salesman</u>. New York: Viking Press, 1975.

Newfield, Jack. <u>Robert Kennedy: A Memoir</u>. New York: E.P. Dutton, 1969.

O'Brien, Tim. <u>The Things They Carried</u>. Boston: Houghton Mifflin, 1990.

O'Connor, Flannery. "A Good Man is Hard to Find." <u>The Story and Its Writer</u>. Ed. Ann Charters. Boston: Bedford/St. Martin. 2003. 658-669. Print.

Oliver, Mary. <u>New and Selected Poems</u>. Boston: Beacon Press, 1992.

Pacheco, Ferdie. <u>Muhammad Ali: A View from the Corner</u>. New York: Birch Lane Press, 1992.

Pomianowski, John. "Funeral Program for Tucker Geery." 22 Jan. 2010.

Remnick, David. <u>King of the World</u>. New York: Vintage Books, 1998.

Shakespeare, William. <u>King Lear</u>. New York: Washington Press, 1993.

"Sixth Inning." Prod. Ken Burns. <u>Baseball</u>. 1994. DVD.

Tennyson, Alfred Lord. "Ulysses." <u>Poems, Poets, Poetry</u>. Helen Vendler. Boston: Bedford Books, 1997.

"Two Towers." Dir. Peter Jackson. New Line Cinema. 2002. DVD.

Valvano, Jimmy. "Espy Awards Speech." The V Foundation for Cancer Research. 4 March 1993. Speech.

Wiesel, Elie. <u>Night</u>. New York: Bantam, 1982.

Wilbur, Richard. <u>The Mind-Reader</u>. New York: Harcourt, Brace, Jovanovich, 1976.

Williams, Tennessee. <u>A Streetcar Named Desire.</u> New York: Signet, 1974.

Paul O'Brien taught English for forty-seven years at Notre Dame and Notre Dame-Bishop Gibbons School. Since leaving the classroom, he has remained active in a number of educational boards including the Notre Dame-Bishop Gibbons School Board, the St. Kateri Tekakwitha School Board, NYSEC, and NYSCEA. His hobbies include reading, writing, traveling, and meeting good friends at the Blue Ribbon Diner for breakfast or lunch. He lives with his wife Deborah in Niskayuna, New York.